Contents

INDEX ON CENSORSHIP

VOLUME 43 NUMBER 02

SUMMER 2014

Culture

92-94 TOOLEY STREET, LONDON SE1 2TH
REGISTERED CHARITY (ENGLAND AND WALES) NO.
325003

EDITOR
RACHAEL JOLLEY
DEPUTY EDITOR
VICKY BAKER
SUB EDITOR
PAUL ANDERSON
CONTRIBUTING EDITORS:
KAYA GENC (TURKEY), NATASHA JOSEPH
(SOUTH AFRICA), JEMIMAH STEINFELD

EDITORIAL ASSISTANT:
Alice Kirkland
THANKS TO: Sean Gallagher, Milana
Knessevic, Padraig Reidy, Richard Miranda,
Matthew Hasteley, Brett Biedscheid

Supported using public funding by
ARTS COUNCIL
ENGLAND

After the fall

by **Rachael Jolley**

EDITORIAL

43(2): 3/4 | DOI: 10.1177/0306422014537953

TWENTY FIVE YEARS ago this autumn the Berlin Wall was pulled down and a wave of euphoria swept not just across that city, but across Europe, and then the world. When, also in 1989, Francis Fukuyama wrote we were seeing the "end of history" it seemed to make sense. His essay suggested not that history was over, but a new era was coming, one in which liberal democracy had defeated authoritarianism and the world would now inevitably become more free.

In the wake of the fall, eastern European nations swapped authoritarian regimes for democratic governments. And people who lived behind that wall were now able to travel more easily, read news that had previously been censored, and listen to music that had been forbidden. Many got the chance to vote in their first free election, with a choice of parties, and even had the option not to vote at all.

Bricks were falling and barriers were coming down as that long line of wire and sentry posts that had divided a continent was dismantled.

A quarter of a century on and the bubble of optimism is deflating. The two world superpowers of the 1980s, the US and Russia, are squaring up again, with presidents Putin and Obama exchanging threats and counter threats. In parts of the former Soviet Union little appears to have changed for the better with attacks on gay people, anti-gay legislation and the introduction of blasphemy and anti-swearing laws. In Belarus and Azerbaijan the hope for freedom still exists, but an atmosphere of fear prevails. Journalists there still live in fear of being beaten up, imprisoned or put under house arrest for writing articles that report problems that dictators would rather not have reported. Internet restrictions stop news being distributed, and *samizdat*, the opposition's underground newspapers of the Soviet era, continues to exist in Belarus. Further west of Moscow things are better than they were. Freedom to travel, write and read what you want came with the new era. But there are ominous signs. In Hungary there has been a rise in discrimination against minority groups such as the Roma, swastikas painted on Jewish gravestones, and a rise in support for fascist groups. In Poland there are similar reports of upsurges in extremism and homophobia. That initial post-wall swell of enthusiasm for change has been replaced by cynicism and anxiety.

Across Europe a strand of nasty nationalism is striding into the political arena. And weeks after Russia occupied Crimea, and continues to stand at the redrawn borders of Ukraine, the European landscape looks almost as anxious and divided as it did in the days of presidents Reagan and Brezhnev. Fears about a new Cold War feel well founded. If history teaches us anything, it should teach us to expect situations to repeat themselves, and to learn from the past.

History is certainly playing a part in these cycles. The narratives of hate often use a rewriting of history to make their case. "Those people hated us, so now we can hate them," argues one set. "They supported the Nazis in the war," argues one more. "The Jews might have had it bad, but it was just as bad for the non-Jewish Poles," argues another. →

ABOVE: Cold war revision - a pro-Russia protester breaks a stone at a barricade in eastern Ukraine in April 2014

Credit: Marko Djurica/Reuters

→ A new memorial to a pro-Nazi leader in Hungary has been erected, and writers with far-right connections are now on the country's school curriculum. Austerity has given the nasty nationalists an opportunity to tell a new story about Europe. It's too open; it's too competitive for jobs; our young people don't have enough opportunities; it's all the fault of (a group can be named here). And all this creates distant echoes of German voices in the 1930s. Austerity and high levels of unemployment open up an angry fear of a troubled future where people will have less than they have now, often an excuse for popular support for repressive legislation. Politicians and wannabe politicians are drawing out emotional memories of Russia's fight against the Nazis; WWII victories; and myths of Russia resplendent in centuries past or Hungary split and defeated, then mixing with nostalgia, a cupful of anger and a return to religiosity, in some cases, to present the case for tighter drawn laws that ban free speech or allow states to clampdown on groups they don't like.

The past is being rewritten.

So, have the expected gains been as nought? In her article for this issue, Irena Maryniak argues that the dividing line in Europe still exists, but it has now shifted further east, along the eastern border of the Baltic states and down the western border of Belarus. To the east there is a greater expectation of conformity and that the group is greater than the individual. There are fault lines where tensions explode and where the push and pull from decades and where arguments about national identity and geopolitical pressures result in sudden uprisings and anger. Meanwhile, Konstanty Gebert, who was a leading Solidarity journalist and continues to work as a writer, charts the public's disillusionment with the "free" press in Poland. He explores why the newly independent media was not as willing to investigate stories as objectively as it should have done, and how people's trust in the media has dissolved.

Our three German writers on the post-wall era explore different themes. Crime writer Regula Venske looks at the expectation that Germany would have a cohesive national identity by now, but her exploration through crime novels of the country's image of itself shows a nation more comfortable with itself as regional rather than national. Matthias Biskupek looks back at theatre and literature censored in the former East Germany; while academic and writer Thomas Rothschild has felt his optimism ebb away. Meanwhile Generation Wall, our panel of under 25-year-olds from eastern Europe, speak to their parents' generation about the past and talk about their present.

Clearly it's not all bad news. Those members of Generation Wall are mentally and physically well travelled in a way that the older generation was not able to enjoy. They have experienced a life mostly uncensored. Freedom House's influential Freedom in the World report shows that the number of countries rated as "free" has swept from 61 to 88, and four more than 1989 are rated "partly free".

And as this year's Eurovision Song Contest showed there are protests across Europe at the heavy handed tactics of Russian authorities, and at their attitudes to minorities. While a Eurovision audience booing at the Russian contestants or Russia's neighbours reducing their traditional 12 votes won't have a long-term effect, it is a sign of an airing of opinions from traditional Russian allies. Bloc voting, so long a tradition in Eurovision, appeared to be breaking down. The end of history has not happened, but learning from the past should never go away. ⊠

© Rachael Jolley
www.indexoncensorship.org

Rachael Jolley is editor of Index on Censorship

If you would like to join the magazine team at our regular debates and launches, please email: davidh@indexoncensorship.org

ABOVE: Former President of Poland Lech Walesa talks to the media at the Fallen Shipyard Workers Monument in Gdansk

SPECIAL REPORT

In this section

Going overground

43(2): 6/10 | DOI: 10.1177/0306422014535895

Poland had the largest alternative press on the eastern side of the Iron Curtain – and journalists couldn't wait for the arrival of democracy. But after its heyday in the early 90s, the Polish media have lost their willingness to take on the powerful, argues **Konstanty Gebert**, who has kept a printing press, just in case   →

TWENTY FIVE YEARS AGO, as the round-table talks in Warsaw between the communist government and the opposition moved forward in the transition to democracy, the courtyard of Warsaw university became a print-lovers' paradise. All kinds of underground publications, from books to newspapers, previously distributed only under the cover of secrecy, circulated in the open, provoking delight, outrage, concern and shock from passers-by. Watching vendors hawking my own publication, the fortnightly KOS – named after the until recently persecuted Komitet Oporu Spolecznego (Committee of Social Resistance) – I grappled with the idea that we might actually become a normal newspaper, sold at newsstands and not in trusted private apart-

We have come to a situation in which readers read little, trust even less, and believe that media have mainly entertainment value at best

ments, competing for newsprint, stories and readers in a free market of commodities and ideas. My only concern was that the promise of liberty would again prove a false dawn. I decided that, if we were to go "overground", we should stash all our printing equipment and supplies somewhere, ready to pick up our clandestine work again if the political situation soured. This, to my eyes, was the greatest threat. Little did I know.

The alternative press had been both the backbone of the underground and one of its most distinctive features: no other communist country had an output that matched Poland's. The Polish National Library has collected almost 6,000 different titles for the years 1976 to 1989 and the estimated number of readers is assessed at anything from 250,000 upwards. In 1987, KOS published

a circular, issued by the regional prosecutor in the provincial industrial town of Płock. It informed his staff that if, during a house search (in a routine criminal investigation, not a political case), no underground publications were found, they needed to assume the inhabitants had been forewarned and had the time to clean up. In other words, the communist state assumed that the absence, not the presence, of underground publications in a typical Polish household was an anomaly that demanded an explanation.

This meant that, when the transition initiated by the round-table talks rushed forward at an unexpectedly speedy pace, we actually had trained journalists ready to take over hitherto state-controlled publications and, more importantly, set up new ones from scratch. The daily Gazeta Wyborcza (the Electoral Gazette was set up to promote Solidarity candidates in the first, semi-free elections of June 1989, but continued beyond that), which proudly advertised itself as the first free newspaper between the Elbe and Vladivostok, became an instant hit. Many formerly underground journalists, including myself, joined the paper, making it, for a while, a collective successor of the entire underground press. Its print run, initially limited by state newsprint allocations to 150,000 copies, soared to 500,000 once the remains of the communist state had been dismantled, and then dropped to under 300,000, as print media lost readers.

The newspaper's unparalleled success (also financial: its publisher Agora went public in 1999 and shares initially did well) was due both to the extraordinary importance attributed under communism to the printed word and to the belief that the paper expressed "the truth" as opposed to "the lie" of the communist media. Under the government's tightly controlled system of public expression (everything, down to matchbox labels, had to clear censorship), reality was defined by what was written, not by what was witnessed.

The underground press described a reality totally at odds with the image presented in the official media, yet validated by everyday experience: it was therefore "true", and this exposed the communists as liars, who, moreover, were powerless to do anything about being exposed, since underground media continued to flourish, police repression notwithstanding. At the same time, the underground press was if not a propaganda venture at least an advocacy one, devoted not to the objective and non-partisan discussion of reality but to the promotion of a political current: the anti-communist opposition. Then we saw no contradiction in considering ourselves independent while supporting Solidarity candidates.

This contradiction was to explode shortly after. In 1990, barely a year after the transformation began, the first democratic presidential elections pitted Solidarity leader Lech Wałesa against his more politically liberal former chief adviser and first non-communist prime minister, Tadeusz Mazowiecki. The unity of the anti-communist movement did not survive the defeat of its adversary – and rightly so. Gazeta Wyborcza endorsed Mazowiecki, to the outrage of many of its readers, even if they, too, voted mainly for the former PM. "Your job," one reader wrote, "is not to tell me how to vote. Your job is to give me information so I can make up my mind myself." The newspaper could no longer count on the uncritical trust of its readers, yet it kept the position of market leader, a rarity for a quality newspaper, until it was dethroned in 2003 by tabloid Fakt.

Gazeta Wyborcza has also become the most reviled paper, at least to its adversaries in the right-wing press. The Wałesa-Mazowiecki split exposed a deep structural fissure inside the anti-communist camp, between the conservative-nationalist Catholics, who endorsed the eventual winner, and the liberal-cosmopolitan secularists, who supported the former PM. As this fissure

grew (deep internal divisions within both camps notwithstanding, and regardless of their shared hostility to the former communists), Gazeta Wyborcza became, in the eyes of the right, the embodiment of an alleged "anti-Polish" project – the fact that editor-in-chief and former political prisoner Adam Michnik is Jewish was sometimes proof enough – that had to be destroyed at all costs. The declining fortunes of the newspaper in recent years have been taken by the right as proof that Poland is now "finally becoming truly independent".

An unexpected challenge came from the former spokesman of the communist government, Jerzy Urban, who in 1990 launched his weekly publication Nie ("no" in Polish). As Urban had been easily the most hated man in Poland, his enterprise was considered doomed in advance by most – and yet

Gazeta Wyborcza and other media were derelict in investigating their friends with the same determination as they investigated the authorities

Nie proved vastly successful, claiming print runs of 300,000 to 600,000 (no independent audit was available, but these estimates are credible). The weekly publication – a mixture of Private Eye-style satire, hard porn, vulgar language and excellent investigative reporting – became an instant hit, because it concentrated on a major area neglected in the anti-communist media: the anti-communists themselves. Gazeta Wyborcza and other new or restructured media had been derelict in their duty of investigating their friends in power with the same determination and mistrust we had previously applied against the communist authorities. This was true of our coverage not only of government, but also of the Catholic church. Remembered as →

ABOVE: People read opposition newspaper Tygodnik Solidarnosc while standing in line at a kiosk in Warsaw, June 1989

→ a victim of communist persecution and as an ally and protector of the underground (even if the reality had been more complex), trusted and revered by the overwhelming majority of the nation, the church was really beyond public criticism. Urban rightly saw in that a potential killing.

And he went after anti-communist ministers and Catholic bishops with a vengeance that struck a chord, not only among the (substantial) former-communist readership, but also among many ordinary readers, who saw in the new authorities more of a continuation of the powers-that-be of old than we would care to admit. Even if uniformly vulgar and occasionally misinformed, his criticisms were painful and to the point. The mainstream media eventually caught up, investigating the secular and ecclesiastical authorities as they should, and, eventually, pushed Urban into a niche of spiteful readers, who appreciate his vulgarity more than his incisiveness; his weekly has a current print run of around 75,000. But it took the twin lessons of the internal political split in Solidarity and the unexpected success of a seemingly compromised propagandist to force mainstream media to understand the basic obligations of their job.

In broadcasting, changes were less dramatic, as there were no trained cadre of independent radio or TV journalists to replace the old hacks: there were hardly any underground broadcast media. More importantly, the new governments, left and right, proved just as reluctant as their predecessors to give up on controlling TV, in the unfounded belief that this helps one win elections. In fact, only one government has been re-elected in the past 25 years, even though all have had as much control over state TV as they wanted and private TV has generally been politically timid. Pressure on radio was much less obvious, and private radio stations have flourished. The most successful one is perhaps Radio Maryja, a Catholic fundamentalist broadcaster, sharply critical of democracy and European integration, and long accused of producing anti-semitic content. From being the object of criticism of the church establishment for its independently extremist line, it has become its de facto mouthpiece: it can get dozens of people out on the street and get MPs elected.

Overall, however, the underground era and the first few years after 1989 were probably the heyday of Polish journalism. But from a high point of newspapers being the visible incarnation of collective political triumph, we have come to a situation when readers read little, trust even less, and believe that media have mainly entertainment value at best, and represent a hostile power run amuck at worst. New media, though immensely popular due to high internet access (53.5 per cent), still run into the problems of bias and low credibility. The printing equipment I had stashed away a quarter-century ago still gathers dust in a Warsaw cellar, its technology as remote from today's electronic potential as the medium it produced is from today's media. ⊠

©Konstanty Gebert
www.indexoncensorship.org

Konstanty Gebert is a Polish journalist. He has worked at Gazeta Wyborcza since 1992 and is the founder of Jewish magazine Midrasz. He was a leading Solidarity journalist, and co-founder of the Jewish Flying University in 1979

ABOVE: A woman chips away at the Berlin Wall, November 1989

Generation Wall

As we approach the 25th anniversary of the Berlin Wall's demolition, Index talks with Generation Wall, young people who have grown up in countries that were behind that division between east and west

Young, free and Polish

GENERATION WALL

43(2): 12/23 | DOI: 10.1177/0306422014539071

Tymoteusz Chajdas discusses Poland past and present, and what freedom means to him and his country

THE DELIVERY OF a package, the size of a small fridge, from abroad was rare in 1980s Poland. My family was fortunate enough to have this privilege. Every month, my two-year-old sister, Joanna, sat on the rubber flooring in the hallway of our two-bedroom apartment. She waited for a package from Jerzy, my uncle who lived in Cologne, West Germany.

The unpacking was always an occasion. But my parents have a particularly strong

> ## "Balls. I've got so many! Come play with me!" It was the first time my two-year-old sister had seen oranges

memory of the first time a package was delivered. When the postman arrived, Joanna opened the box and immediately started playing with the contents. "Balls. I've got so many! Come play with me!" It was the first time my sister had seen oranges.

This was the reality of that time. Poland became isolated from the rest of Europe when the Soviets erected the Berlin Wall in 1961. The ideals of liberty, freedom and democracy remained unattainable for an average Pole for the next 28 years. Some only experienced these ideals remotely by having family in the West, and occasionally receiving "samples" of what Western life was like.

Over on the eastern side of the wall, Poles couldn't buy basic material goods easily, such as food or hygiene products. Large chunks of everyday life consisted of tedious searches and hours standing in long lines to buy essentials. Store shelves were frequently empty, and it seemed the only item always in stock was vinegar. Even if a product was available, it could only be purchased upon presentation of a ration card.

"Jerzy was devastated by this," says my mother, Jadwiga, talking about her brother. In 1979, my uncle was invited by a friend for a three-week holiday in the Netherlands. After two weeks, Jerzy decided to stay on the other side of the wall. He applied for political asylum and never came back.

"He could stay there under one condition: he had to reject Polish citizenship," she tells me. "So he did. Within two years he started sending us food and clothing."

A few years later, another relative of ours emigrated to the United States. While the Berlin Wall divided Europe into two worlds,

Poles could not reveal any connections they had with the West. It was around this time my father started his career at the Silesian Police Department.

"We started to fear our own shadows," says my mother, remembering that having family in the West was both a blessing and curse. Any association with capitalist Europe posed a threat to the authorities of communist Poland and was seen as political espionage and violation of the communist ideology. "[Your father] had to renounce family members living in the West if he wanted to stay employed," says my mother. "Our phone was tapped so we had little contact with them."

Despite this, my family still received packages. Only those who worked two jobs or were communist party members could afford to live comfortably, so my mother had to lie about her income to cover up for the extra goods we received from relatives abroad.

Less privileged Poles had little or no understanding of what life looked like on the other side of the Iron Curtain. Jolanta Sudy, a high school teacher and family friend, remembers those times very well. She says the majority of Poles were victims of communist propaganda and were unaware of what was happening in their own country.

"As far as censorship is concerned, the Soviets presented the Eastern Bloc as an El Dorado where everything was perfect and no problems existed," she says. The government spread its ideology through newspapers, magazines, books, films and theatre productions. Popular radio and television broadcasts were also censored and reinforced the views of the communist party.

Every year on 1 May, all Polish citizens were obliged to attend a street parade celebrating the International Worker's Day. A register of attendance was kept. "It looked like a country fair or circus," recalls Sudy. "Everyone was dressed up to show how joyful it was to live in Poland, how happy we were because of the socialist system. But the party stood above us with a whip."

The elections worked similarly and attendance was also mandatory. Many saw them as an ironic spectacle organised by the authorities. The ballot paper featured only one name. "I always signed the register but I never put the card in the box," says Sudy. "This was my battle with communism."

Such oppression, constant fear and invigilation had a strong influence on the Poles. Some listened to Radio Free Europe, which broadcast unbiased news from Western countries.

In 1989 the situation changed drastically: the Berlin Wall was torn down.

"The store shelves filled up again with foreign goods," says my mum. "Travel agents started organising vacations to other countries. This was very difficult before then."

An invisible wall divides us into those who are too young to remember and those who suddenly woke up in a capitalist country

Some Poles found the change shocking. Sudy says that, after the fall of the Berlin Wall, the amount of uncensored news was overwhelming. "It was hard to believe that we could have lived differently since the end of World War II."

The overturn of the uniform culture of communist Poland gave birth to a cultural explosion which had skillfully been repressed by the Soviets. Free expression in the arts in Poland did not exist during the communist period, according to Kasia Gasinska, a 24-year-old graphic designer. Some Polish citizens listened to music from non-authorised radio stations but it was only "after the wall fell down that [Polish] art became liberated," recalls Gasinska.

→   Gasinska says that Western music suddenly became available in Poland, and Poles set up new bands. "New music genres were introduced, such as rave or techno, which embodied the feeling of freedom shared by many at the time."

The collapse of communism also brought with it one of the most powerful artistic forms – street art, says Gasinska. Many Poles

Some Poles found the change shocking. After the fall of the wall, the amount of uncensored news was overwhelming

made the journey to the remnants of the Berlin Wall where they could freely express themselves through graffiti.

This expanded as an artistic movement to major cities in Poland. Lodz, the third largest city and a post-industrial centre, became one of many hubs for street art, famous for its colourful murals and playful graffiti that covered many bleak estates.

Polish cinema was liberated from communist propaganda as well. There were new movies that referred to the Polish romantic ideals of the previous epoch, as well as comedies and films that dealt with everyday life in the wake of the political transformation.

Today, the events that led to the dismantling of the Berlin Wall seem like a distant memory for many young Poles, myself included. I was born in 1990 and I only learnt about those times by listening to the stories my parents told. Some were scary, some funny. But mostly, they feel unreal, as does the idea of getting shot at for attempting to cross the western border.

Although the Berlin Wall was torn down 25 years ago, divisions can still be felt. An invisible wall divides us into those who are too young to remember and those who suddenly woke up in a capitalist country. Some made up for the lost time and found themselves in the new system. Others still tend to talk about the good old communist times when the pace of life was less hectic.

But even these Poles wouldn't deny that the Berlin Wall has become a symbol of an unrealistic system, gradual economic decline and political oppression. Today, its ruins

GENERATION WALL

Fighting for history
....

As other members of the Eastern Bloc flourished after the fall of the wall, the former Yugoslavia spiralled into disrepair, says our Generation Wall reporter **Milana Knezevic**

My father used to work as a cameraman for Bosnian television. On the day the Berlin Wall came down he was in their central Sarajevo newsroom watching it unfold live. "We were all cheering," he says. The mood was good, initially. They were happy that Germany was reuniting. It was only later that they started to consider

the other consequences.

One of my aunt's strongest memories was seeing how pleased the whole of Europe was: "We thought East Germany was now going to blossom." Beyond that, however, it was not an occasion that left a huge mark. "There weren't any noticeable changes in everyday life," she explains. "I'm sure there

was a shift on the political level, but it did not have a day-to-day impact on the population." My mother barely even recalls the day the wall came down.

"For me, a much bigger occasion was the day President Tito died," recalls my aunt, with a smile. "I thought the Russians were going to attack straight away. I

remind me of the adversities many eastern Europeans had to go through to experience living in a free, democratic country. Few remember that, at the time, only hope kept the Poles dreaming of a better life.

My mother told me that when she was a child, she received a present from her friend who was leaving for West Germany. "It was a pair of knee-high socks with blue and red stripes at the top. Today, I would say they were unsightly," she says. "But back then, I wore them every day. Every time I looked at them, I promised myself that it was going to be better one day." ☒

Tymoteusz Chajdas, 23, grew up in Bytom, Poland. He is a freelance journalist and a recent graduate of the journalism school at Cardiff University

---

remember running home, waiting for the planes."

Of course, the fall of the wall was not the most significant event of the decade for Yugoslavia. Less than two years after this historic act of demolition, the dissolution of the federation was under way. Volumes have been devoted to the reasons behind it, with the fight for the country's history continuing long after the weapons were laid down. In hindsight, it is difficult to argue against the destabilising impact caused by the total breakdown of recognised world order – most obviously symbolised by the fall of the Berlin Wall – on the already fragile union. According to my father, the intelligentsia knew that this would have an impact on Yugoslavia.

War is the ultimate deprivation of freedom. The issue of freedom in the region since the war has been complicated, for lack of a better word. My family were relatively lucky as we escaped Sarajevo relatively early and settled in idyllic Norway when I was three years old. Hundreds →

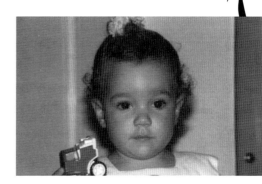

ABOVE: Milana Knezevic as a toddler

→ of thousands of others fared much, much worse.

Every now and then, I do experience that pull towards a home and a culture I never truly had the chance to call my own; a sort of immigrant-kid blues. However, I recognise that I am overwhelmingly privileged compared to many of my peers who stayed behind. Among the countless ways this privilege manifests itself, is the opportunity to observe the former Yugoslavia from the outside. I can use many words to describe what I see. Freedom is not one of them.

Twenty-five years after the fall of the wall, corruption on an endemic scale hinders any chance of meaningful growth in eastern Europe. A partisan and cowed popular press denies large sections of the public access to reliable information. The rights of minorities, notably Roma and LGBT people, continue to be trampled. Doesn't sound much like freedom, does it?

In this context, special attention must be paid to Bosnia. Without dismissing the struggles they continue to face, most of the former republics have made some progress.

Bosnia, meanwhile, has stagnated. Some might say this is to be expected. After all, Bosnia was torn asunder in a way the others simply weren't. But after the war, a cocktail of misguided state-building and opportunist, nationalist and corrupt politicians have seen the country frozen in a post-conflict no man's land for 20 years. Ethnicity-based separation was written into the constitution formed in the 1995 Dayton peace accords. This has manifested itself in a variety of ways, from a tripartite Bosniak-Croat-Serb presidency to segregated schools. The situation has been utilised by leaders in a cynical game of divide and conquer. While Bosnia may not have slid back, it has not had the chance to move on.

Among the biggest losers are Bosnia's young people. My generation have been deprived of opportunities most of, if not all, their lives. Recent figures put youth unemployment at a staggering 63.1 per cent. A 2013 survey found that 81 per cent would leave tomorrow if given the choice. That's not what freedom looks like to me.

Had I been writing this in 2013, that's probably where it would have ended. As chance would have it, however, the 25th anniversary of the fall of the wall looks like it could be a year of change for Bosnia. Protests, peaceful but for pockets of vandalism, suddenly swept the nation this past February. The closure of yet

A 2013 survey found that 81 per cent would leave tomorrow if given the choice. That's not what freedom looks like to me

another factory in the former industrial hub Tuzla was the spark. The flame spread and was sustained by the legitimate anger at the fundamental mismanagement of the country over 20 years, from both young and old. Let down by the political establishment and the failed strategies of the international community, the Bosnian people have taken matters into their own hands. A number of local governments, including the one in Sarajevo, have been overthrown and replaced by citizen assemblies, open for anyone to attend. The images from the meetings, spread across social media, are a remarkable sight and represent direct democracy in action.

Bosnia has seen protests before, but never on this scale and never sustained for so long. With people still taking to the street daily across the country, the momentum is showing no signs of petering out anytime soon. The past 25 years have not brought with them much in the way of freedom for the Bosnian people. While I remain cautious of making sweeping conclusions, recent events give cause for cautious optimism that the next 25 will. ⌧

© Milana Knezevic
www.indexoncensorship.org

Milana Knezevic, 23, was born in Sarajevo, Bosnia. She is an editorial assistant at Index on Censorship

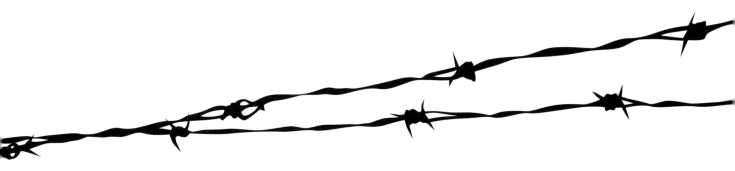

Talking about my generation

GENERATION WALL

43(2): 12/23 | DOI: 10.1177/0306422014539071

Ivett Körösi recalls her childhood in democratic Hungary and interviews her parents about the struggles of previous generations

THIS SPRING HUNGARY held free and democratic elections for the sixth time since the country's transition to democracy in 1990. A few months ago a friend of mine told me that he would not cast his vote. "I'm not a big fan of any of the parties. I don't agree with any of them, so I'd rather not go," he said, adding that his parents were outraged by the idea of him not voting.

They believe it is a citizen's obligation to vote and thus influence the future. It is understandable: living in socialist Hungary, life was quite different for our parents. While we were able to choose from twenty-something political parties, they mostly had one candidate on their ballots.

Having plenty of opportunities is natural for members of my generation. We, who are in our late 20s and early 30s, have known nothing but democracy. We grew up watching Disney cartoons, dancing to the latest music videos on MTV, learning a variety of foreign languages (not Russian like our parents), travelling and often living abroad. There are no obstacles in front of us – apart from money, as in all capitalist countries.

Not so long ago things were dramatically different. Although the Hungarian regime was the least harsh among the countries of the Eastern Bloc, possibilities were very limited and the future did not appear too bright.

"In the 70s and early 80s it seemed impossible that the regime could change. No one ever thought that this could happen,"

We grew up travelling and learning a variety of foreign languages (not just Russian like our parents)

says my father, 57-year-old Tamas Körösi, while telling me about his youth. "We just accepted our fate, that through all our lifetimes the Hungarian Socialist Workers' Party (MSZMP) would rule the country. We didn't try to change anything, we only tried to make our own ways in life."

He admits that politics was never a topic of conversation at the dinner table, so he started to question the status quo quite →

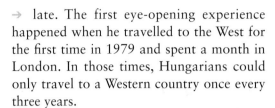

→ late. The first eye-opening experience happened when he travelled to the West for the first time in 1979 and spent a month in London. In those times, Hungarians could only travel to a Western country once every three years.

My dad says: "It was completely different from everything I had come across before. It was like being on another planet. People also

For any journalist who took his job seriously, the transition to democracy was liberating

looked at me as if I was an alien. They kept asking me about the Soviets in Hungary. I felt embarrassed and tried to justify certain things although I knew that the system was unjustifiable."

His eyes still shine as he tells me about London. Being in a Western metropolis was not only strange but irritating at the beginning since there were so many new things. "I only processed the whole experience after I got home. Then I started to realise that things could be different. I was still amazed by what I saw in London: the colourful multitude of people; the variety of products on the shelves; the professional attitude of businesses."

He had to wait more than 10 years to see the same in Hungary. After Mikhail Gorbachev was appointed as general secretary of the Communist Party of the Soviet Union in 1985, he initiated widespread reforms and an opening of the system, known as *glasnost* and *perestroika*. Soon, the pillars of the old regime started to shake, affecting the rest of the Eastern Bloc, including Hungary.

By 1989, the iconic leader of the country János Kádár had been retired for a year, and some reformers rose high in MSZMP. They started to negotiate with the opposition and in 1990 the first democratic elections were

BELOW: Ivett Korsoi as a child

held. My father describes that period as constant euphoria.

"You could breathe freely, the air suddenly became fresh. The pressure of the socialist ideology was gone: the times when you could only say what you were expected to, were gone," he says, adding that the changes that took place in the media, the emergence of different voices, were also refreshing.

The sudden freedom of speech was not only welcomed by newspaper readers, but even more by journalists. Gabor Miklós has been working at the newspaper Népszabadság for almost four decades. The national daily had been the party's official newspaper until the transition. Miklós says that the press in socialist Hungary was relatively free compared to the rest of the Eastern Bloc. However, there were some rules journalists knew should be obeyed: the party's leader could not be criticised nor could the relations with the Soviet Union. "If you are part of a system and you don't want to quit, you know how to write in such a way that a piece is publishable."

The articles, however, went through a thorough supervision, and a text could be checked by up to 12 editors. "They didn't say they checked the pieces for political reasons, but for professional ones: to avoid sloppiness and inaccuracy." But many journalists at Népszabadság were highly skilled writers and, according to Miklós, often managed to write in a way that could help an observant reader understand the meanings between the lines.

The troubled 80s had a big impact on the press as well. Just like in politics, some people wanted to follow the path of the reforms, while others were more cautious. "This was a very troubled and exciting period. Those who worked at Népszabadság started to feel that the newspaper was not only losing readers but it was also losing the prestige it had before. If you went to a press conference, you could feel that other journalists drew away from you."

He remembers it as a period of much anxiety and although he continued to work for the newspaper he joined Openness Club, an alternative group whose members gathered to draft manifestos and to talk freely about current issues. His superiors at Népszabadság threatened to sack him soon after he joined the alternative group, but the reporter refused.

Miklós, who still works at Népszabadság – which has been privatised after the transition and, since then, has become an independent and critical voice – says: "For any journalist who took his job seriously, the transition to democracy was a liberating experience."

For my generation, this is all history. Although we were born before the collapse of the Eastern Bloc, by the time we were old enough to understand the world that surrounded us, socialism was swept out. Streets and institutions that had been named after socialist icons – such as Lenin Boulevard and the Karl Marx University of Economics – were re-named, new history books were published and the symbols of socialist ideology were gone.

Of course, people often talked about "the old system", it was also a point of reference in politics. But we never had to experience anything like our parents did. Although it was a fresh democracy and Hungary had much to catch up with compared to other democratic countries, we did not experience any vestiges of socialism, only freedom, and a wide range of rights and possibilities in front of us.

In a way, we have been spoiled and left naïve, which can be a dangerous thing: we never really had to fight for what we have. However, that could all be about to change as rights we took for granted, especially those with regards to freedom of expression, might soon be under threat.

The widely criticised new media law – which the current government claims is in line with European standards – was passed

ABOVE: People gathered to rally for reforms at Alexanderplatz, East Berlin, November 1989

four years ago and has been changed several times since then. It created a regulatory body that is not independent from the government. It can impose a range of excessive sanctions on media organisations, based on subjective criteria regarding content and breaches not clearly defined in the law. Many international actors, including the European Council, claimed that this could result in self-censorship and called it a threat to freedom of expression.

As a journalist, I have never experienced any barriers in my work, and I never want to. This is a wake-up call for all of us, the spoiled and naïve youth: is time to look back and learn from the past. ⊠

© Ivett Korsoi
www.indexoncensorship.org

Ivett Korosi, 26, is a foreign affairs journalist who grew up in Budapest, Hungary

Perpetual transition

....

Bulgaria is still a country in flux since the fall of the Berlin Wall, both politically and culturally, says **Victoria Pavlova**

Bulgaria had little popular culture to speak of in the years after 1989, with the death of dissidence and resistance art, music and literature.

Bulgaria is still a country in flux. The process of finding its political footing has been a long and painful one, even 25 years after the country's communist leader Todor Zhivkov was ousted from power. However, Bulgaria is a prime example of a nation where political turmoil has been symptomatic of major cultural shifts among its inhabitants.

Outside the political sphere, the move away from the socialist regime has been much more subtle and, arguably, more difficult. Bulgaria does not have millenials, the term regularly used for the generation of those born between the 1980s and 2000s.

Instead, it has the "children of the transition", referring to the period of reconstruction following the fall of the Zhivkov regime. However, no one knows exactly what the transition entails or how long it is supposed to last. As far as most Bulgarians are concerned the country is still in the middle of this era.

In the eyes of the older generation, those born after 1989 are confused, lack a strong moral core and a cause to stand for. Family friend Todor Yovchev 43, is one of the many who have voiced objections against the new state of things. "A lot of things were better then than they are now," he says. "The food was cheaper. There was less crime."

Slobodiya (freedom without equivalent responsibility) was a term I grew up hearing. In a sense it means too much freedom or too much

choice; an odd concept for me and my democratically raised friends. For the older generation, there is comfort in discipline and the familiarity of the socialist routine. Socialist life might have lacked opportunity, but it also came without the fear of uncertainty. This goes some way to explaining feelings of nostalgia for the 1980s, despite it being a period marked by significant economic slowdown, debt to foreign banks and frequent energy shortages. Those who are nostalgic about the regime believe my generation, the children of the transition, to be spoiled by choice, apathetic and undisciplined. As my father Valentin Pavlov, 49, says: "This generation cares about nothing so they'll get nowhere."

Yet these are the same young people who, after the original wave of protests last summer

began to fizzle out, organised and maintained occupations across the country often under the threat of violence. Students had a strong presence throughout, often ceasing lectures in many of Bulgaria's

institutions through sit-ins. A peaceful protest in Sofia University lasted for 24 days in October and November 2013, and was covered by national radio, television and print media.

It is my generation, the millenials, who are changing this. They are doing so away from formalised spaces and the spectacle of media formats, preferring the street and private gatherings.

At the same time, young people "with potential" are leaving the country. Census results are depressing to say the least. Speaking with my peers, roughly one in five high school students

Bulgaria does not have millenials, the term regularly used for those born between the 1980s and 1990s. Instead it has "the children of the transition"

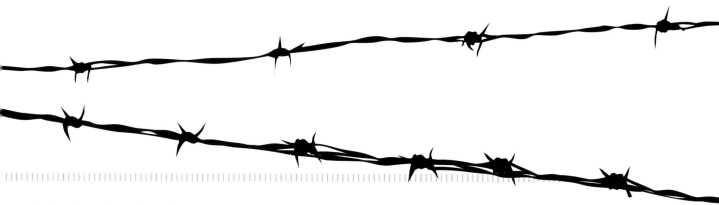

is planning to leave the country and study elsewhere. Some of them have told me they plan to come back, eventually.

However, many of those who have taken the leap to study abroad are now beginning to feel the pull to return to their home country. "I couldn't live anywhere else," says Sofiya Vasileva, a second-year student at a UK university. She is one of many.

Blogs and websites, which were slow to enter the mass consciousness at first, have become widely used news sources and spaces for discussion in the last five years. Social media is where people gather and organise. During last year's protests the movement formed around the social media hashtag #ДАНСwithme. This play on words drew together the famous phrase "dance with me" with the abbreviated name of the National Security Agency.

The prominent desire among my generation is for change. Only a decade ago desperation was still thick in the air, but those who grew up during the transition era are now eager to help create a new, cultural Bulgaria. In the end, there is no roadmap for the "transition". It may be that it needs to be a constant process. But as those born after 1989 are becoming more and more active in all areas of public life, the renewed will to defy emigration statistics and succeed at home is becoming the defining characteristic of a generation. ☒

© Victoria Pavlova
www.indexoncensorship.
org

Victoria Pavlova (pictured left, as a child) is a freelance writer, vlogger and third-year Sociology and English student at the University of Leeds. She grew up in Varna, Bulgaria

Enemies of the people

43(2): 24/27 | DOI: 10.1177/0306422014535686

Writer **Matthias Biskupek** took part in demonstrations in East Germany as the Berlin Wall came down. He looks back at the attempts to censor books and theatre

LET'S FIRST CALL to mind that radical change that took place 25 years ago in the heart of Germany. At that time, it was a firmly divided organ – on one side Berlin, the capital of East Germany; on the other, West Berlin, the three free sectors.

In summer 1989, the East German state, the German Democratic Republic, was already starting to teeter: its leader had taken refuge in his illness, while his subjects, who were eager to be mature citizens, left via Hungary or the Western embassies – or shouted: "We're staying here!" These public voices were not in the majority, even if there were 70,000 of them in Leipzig on 9 October. There was, however, an overwhelming majority of up to 90 per cent who simply wanted to stay in the country they had always lived in.

During that October, the cry was: "We are the people!" It was a riposte to the strictly regulated official newspapers' description of the demonstrators as "enemies of the people". This was long before we started hearing Chancellor Helmut Kohl's slogan "We are one people!" – and it came from citizens who had previously been very well behaved and were often loyal to the state.

It was no coincidence that the largest demonstration in Berlin's history, held on Alexanderplatz on 4 November, was organised by artists: actors, songwriters, authors and painters. One of their principal demands was: "Abolish censorship!" – although there had already been an official decree to this effect for the book trade. More of that later.

When, five days after this demonstration, the wall didn't fall, but was rendered ridiculous in true bureaucratic German style, with every identification card presented there being waved through, there was nothing left for authors to do but what they had been doing all along: write down their stories, ideas, desires and impressions.

People who had only ever written to oppose the authorities' power began to wonder what they could now be asked to do. But very quickly a new power emerged – accommodating and centuries-old – the power of a free market for publishing.

In East Germany itself, "censorship" had always been a word shrouded in mystery, a word that at one time would always crop up in the discussion following a public reading. People would ask the author, in loud voices, whether the book had been censored. There was a hunger for truth – and people believed they found it in authors. They were seen as prophets who could answer the basic question: "How should you live in a state that is not very pleasant?"

Perhaps authors represented their own experiences in a different, more balanced and forceful way than the usual fare served up by the newspapers. Or so a lot of people believed. The possibility of discovering true life while living under a false ideology was the reason the latest books flew off the shelves, and why people kept going to readings. Publicity was generated in interminable all-night conversations in the fug of Prenzlauer Berg kitchen-diners in Berlin. For many people, books and the wisdom they proclaimed were bread-and-butter necessities. And since the cost of bread, butter and everything else was so low, even somebody who was just starting out, and had no real contacts in the East German government, could make a living as a freelance artist. But were you a true poet if your work was published officially, and was therefore permitted? This kind of thinking still overshadows every word published in the former East Germany.

Let's explore this by looking at a book in detail. Siegfried Lokatis, a professor of book studies in Leipzig, has often demonstrated that he doesn't evaluate books from a present-day perspective. He simply asks: "What was it like back then?", "What was written?", "What was published?", "Who did what, and when?". He put together the 350-page paperback Vom Autor zur Zensurakte – Abenteuer im Leseland DDR (From Author to Censor's File – Adventures in the Land of Books) with Theresia Rost and Grit Steuer. There are thick black lines on the cover, as well as the words "confidential" and "report". This is the average person's idea of censorship: it's mainly a case of putting black lines through things; a quaint, almost romantic notion.

The papers collected in this book – mostly by students of publishing history, who often have no first-hand experience of East Germany – chart the history of censorship measures in various decades since 1950. But it is important to remember that when talking about censorship in East Germany, you must always ask: "When?" Things were different just after the war from how they were in the

ABOVE: Author Christoph Hein gives a speech during a rally at Alexanderplatz in East Berlin, 4 November 1989

world of books. Cabaret programmes that had previously been sanctioned, but which a single citizen suddenly found provocative and "reported", would suddenly have to be performed before a selected audience, prefer-

But were you a true poet if your work was published officially?

ably in the morning, at an unusual hour for cabaret. If the reaction was a stony silence, the authorities could then tell the performers: "Your programme doesn't work! The people are not amused! Wouldn't you prefer to cancel it voluntarily?" Of course, you always followed this paternal advice.

In 1983, I experienced one of these reactions to a programme for which I was →

ABOVE: Protesters around Alexanderplatz in Berlin, November 1989. The banners read: "once a liar, always a liar ..." and "democracy"

Credit: dpa picture alliance/Alamy

→ responsible, in the Fettnäppchen cabaret in Gera. There was an unwritten rule for East German cabaret programmes that between the skits that addressed "mistakes, weaknesses and shortcomings" – an ironic

The know-all attitude of the East German evaluators, who were supposed to be literature experts, still fills their former victims with rage

term for all those little niggles, like gaps in the supply chain or poor transport links – there had to be at least one "West number" that pilloried the inhumanity of capitalism, agitprop style. There is something similiar to the "West number" from Author to Censor's File: a piece about the blocking of Luchterhand's proposed edition of Anna Seghers's 1936 novel The Seventh Cross. The blockers were cold warriors from the West.

However, the know-all attitude of the East German evaluators, who were supposed to be independent literature experts, still fills their former victims with rage. One fundamental evil of the East German state was that it handed down judgments on what was good and right, from the battlements of a "vanguard of the proletariat". They dictated when the people should read Franz Kafka, and when Norwegian poems were opportune. This did more to damage citizens' trust in the state than any "evil Bonn ultra" – an ironic term for Western cold warriors.

But when we read books about censorship in East Germany, we are also prompted to think about current practices. In the 1995 book Fragebogen: Zensur (Questionnaire: Censorship), edited by US academic Richard Zipser, the East German author John Erpenbeck complains that "no form of censorship is so devastating, so damaging to personalities and to literature as a whole, as the brute censorship of the market".

Cautiously, we may object that censorship has actually been an extra-economic practice since the time of the sainted Prince Metternich. Today's practices of refusing to publish or pay attention, of denial and exclusion, can be overcome a little more easily (with the help of the internet, for example) than censorship during the epoch of the printed book, a medium that began to lose its dominance around the same time as the fall of East Germany.

Censorship and editing – and the latter also includes the rejection of texts for reasons of quality and taste – are two very different things, as can be illustrated using a short sentence from Lokatis's anthology. When a 25-year-old author writes about a "notorious petition against the exile of the critical songwriter Wolf Biermann in 1976", you might suggest to him that it is possibly the exile, and not the petition, that is notorious. But the Hauptverwaltung Verlage und Buchhandel certainly wouldn't have stopped the young author using this expression.

So was it possible to publish one's opinion anywhere after the fall of the Berlin Wall? Was that time a good time for unpublished manuscripts? "No", many authors would say today, because then those pitiless market rules took over, taking away the market for some writers. And not just upstanding (mendacious) party authors, either.

But I had no problem being published from north to south, east to west, and for the first time was also able to try out my abilities as a polemical journalist. Was I an exception? After 1990, clichéd categories developed that still exist today: here the Germans, there the East Germans; here East German authors, there German authors.

Even so, after 1989 many East Germans began to feel a certain sense of superiority, in contrast to the widespread media image of them as moaning *Ossis* (Easties), the losers of German reunification.

Seasoned East Germans take their superior viewpoint – if they have one – from a sense of having survived: they have already witnessed the collapse of a state. They know the catastrophe that others live in fear of is already behind them. They know that when a miracle happens and something long-established comes crashing down, it's not all bad. In the 1970s and 1980s, East Germans experienced the sensation that now grips the masses of unified Germany: the state is finished. But for individuals with a private income, things are mighty fine. ("Mighty fine, Egon!" was the victory cry of the East's cult film gangsters, the Olsen Gang, when they got one over on the lazy state of Denmark.)

Then as now: the holes are patched over, and the people placated with speeches. Humour and self-deprecation help, and a degree of pragmatism is the most helpful thing of all: you just have to muddle through, or *durchwurschteln*, as they say in Saxony. Many people, including all kinds of writers, were not especially courageous through the hard times of East German censorship. But they always muddled through.⊠

@Matthias Biskupek
www.indexoncensorship.org

Matthias Biskupek grew up in East Germany. He has been a freelance author and journalist since 1983, and has more than three dozen books to his name

Judging Prague's democratic difficulties

43(2): 28/32 | DOI: 10.1177/0306422014538156

Twenty five years after communist rule, former presidential adviser **Jiri Pehe** considers the struggle for public belief in the Czech state

IN THE LAST 25 years, Czech democracy, just like other new democracies in east-central Europe, has undergone an unprecedented institutional modernisation. Yet, it still shows significant democratic deficits. The problem has to do mainly with the fact that the quality of democracy can be judged on two different levels: institutions and culture.

The institutional modernisation has been in part accelerated by assistance and expertise from international organisations, such as the EU. Developing a democratic culture however takes much longer and has to do with the quality of civil society.

Democratic behaviour, rooted in active citizenship, cannot be instituted from above. The creation of a truly democratic environment is tied to people's ability to internalise democratic values, which, in turn, is closely tied to the growth of a civil society.

Tomas Garrigue Masaryk, the first president of an independent Czechoslovakia created after World War I, was well aware of this dilemma. He famously said: "Now that we have a democracy, what we also need are democrats."

Unfortunately, most post-1989 politicians did not realise that democracy is not just a collection of mechanisms, procedures and institutions, but is also a question of culture.

That culture, in turn, is dependent on the quality of civil society. The politicians did not understand that institutional modernisation needed to apply to the state and was not just about creating a political democracy and a market economy.

The era of democracy building after 1989 was, from the beginning, saddled with the popular notion that the state was corrupt, inefficient and oppressive, because that was how the state was perceived during communism. After communism, the state was portrayed by the political elite, mesmerised by the notion of "the invisible hand of the market", as an essentially hostile institution, which should be as small as possible.

One could argue that even a small state could be efficient. The traditions of a deep public distrust of the state, however, combined with a neo-liberal philosophy, which preferred privatising rather than modernising important state functions, conspired to maintain a state with which most Czechs do not identify, even 25 years after the fall of communism.

Part of the problem with the rather significant gap that exists between the quickly established institutions of a political democracy and a market economy, on the one hand, and a still struggling democratic culture, on

ABOUT: People in Prague's Wenceslas Square hold candles and the national flag in tribute to former Czech President Vaclav Havel after his death in 2011. Havel, a dissident playwright, was jailed under communism and later led the bloodless Velvet Revolution

the other, paradoxically has to do with a "return to Europe", one of the most important and widely shared expectations of anti-communist revolutions of 1989.

Unlike Czechoslovakia during its first republic (1918-1938), the newly emerged democracies in east-central Europe were, in 1989, surrounded by democratic countries. These countries were eager (both individually and also through international organisations) to assist the region with building democracy. They also wanted to integrate the region as quickly as possible into supranational organisations, such the European Union and Nato.

Both western Europe and the United States engaged in a massive transfer of know-how, providing at the same time active guidance in democracy and market economy building in the region. If we judge the results of these efforts only on the merits of the achieved

institutional transformation, the change has been spectacular.

In fact, we could argue that it was a historically unprecedented development. Nowhere in the history of the world were so many countries with previously backward-looking and authoritarian political institutions, transformed so quickly into modern democratic regimes with market economies, where the rule of law prevails.

However, the speed of this institutional transformation, culminating in countries joining Nato and the EU, has had some drawbacks. It created an even larger gap between the new institutional reality, and democracy understood as culture. In other words, the very rapid institutional modernisation has intensified the problem of "democracies without democrats".

The negative consequences of this development are numerous. The new democracies

→ in east-central Europe suffer from a highly confrontational political environment and a political scene, which is sharply polarised. The culture of dialogue and reaching compromises is still very underdeveloped.

Mental attitudes from the communist era remain strong. Some analysts speak about "a Bolshevik mentality", which could be best described with communist era slogans, such as "either you're with us or against us". This mentality is characterised by a high degree of intolerance towards others with different views: political opponents are not to be listened to, they have to be destroyed.

Reforms that have taken place in the last 25 years can be best analysed in four interconnected areas: the creation of democratic

The very rapid institutional modernisation has intensified the problem of "democracies without democrats"

political institutions and processes; the transformation of state-planned economies into market economies; the gradual introduction of the rule of law; and the growth of a civil society.

The creation of democratic political institutions and processes was, in relative terms, the easiest of the four difficult tasks. There had been "cookbooks" in the form of the already existing democratic systems in the West and, in some cases, pre-communist political traditions. Institutional and political changes, such as staging free elections or introducing the necessary constitutional frameworks, could be achieved "from above", by adopting the necessary legislative measures or, in some cases, by government decree.

The transformation of state-planned economies into market economies was a more difficult task, because the functioning of a market economy depends even more heavily than the functioning of political institutions

on non-institutional factors. In other words, the notion of a market economy cannot be reduced to privatisation and free competition. If it is to function properly it needs to be recognised as a form of civil society based on certain virtues, ethical rules and respect for laws.

The purely institutional efforts to privatise and reform the economy were also very complex, taking on different forms. They ranged from traditional methods, such direct sales of state assets to both domestic and foreign investors, to more experimental ones, such as Czechoslovakia's voucher privatisation. Various post-communist states also used, to varying degrees, the restitution of assets to owners and their descendants whose property had been expropriated by the communists as a way to privatise what was in public ownership.

The introduction of the rule of law has been even more difficult than political and economic modernisation, because the rule of law is heavily dependent not only on the quality of legislation and institutions, such as the courts, but also on the ability of people to respect the law. Not surprisingly, it eventually became clear that good institutions and laws do not suffice to build the rule of law; law-abiding citizens are equally important. Respect for the law is directly tied to the maturity of civil society.

Indeed, the most difficult area to reform, is civil society, where immaturity means the democratic culture remains underdeveloped. Civil society cannot really be created from above by laws, decrees or by adopting EU legal standards. It is an organism that needs to grow from below, from the grass-roots.

In other words, a robust civil society is a precondition for the internalisation of democratic values. The proper functioning of the system of liberal democracy is based not only on the existence of democratic institutions and appropriate constitutional frameworks but also on individuals' ability to respect democratic values and rules.

The transition to liberal democracy in the Czech Republic has taken place amid the accelerating process of globalisation, which calls into question the very notion of the nation state, the foundation upon which liberal democracy first developed. So, the Czechs are struggling not only with internally generated problems, but with dilemmas created by supranational integration, and by changes in the very paradigm of liberal democracy. The declining role of traditional political parties is an example of this, as is the growing influence of the media on democratic systems.

The most important Czech political parties were created after 1989 by small groups of newly born elites. Even some of the historic political parties, such as the Česká strana sociálně demokratická (ČSSD – Social Democratic Party) were re-established as basically elite projects.

In combination with a high level of mistrust among citizens in partisanship after more than 40 years of one-party rule, the creation of parties as elite projects has caused them to be small and weak. There are no mass parties now to speak of. In fact, the communist party, Komunistická strana Čech a Moravy (KSČM), which inherited a large membership base, still remains the largest party in Czech politics.

The fact that such small and weak parties presided over an extensive privatisation process caused the parties themselves to be "privatised". Leading parties played a crucial role in creating the new entrepreneurs and the powerful economic groups that dominated the newly privatised economy. They then, because of their internal weaknesses, became not only intertwined with the new economic actors but also dependent on them.

Today, Czech political parties often act more as business entities trading political influence than defenders of public interests. High levels of corruption are prevalent because political parties are often controlled by behind-the-scenes economic interests.

When the privatisation process, which was a source of major corruption, ended, many of the newly created business interests used their close contacts with political parties to manipulate the state tendering process and win large contracts. The influence of big money on political parties, has, of course, been a problem in all democratic societies, but the kind of mass parties with long independent traditions that still exist in the West have been able to resist the dictate of big money better than the weak, "privatised" parties in the Czech Republic.

Czech democracy has further been crippled by the fact that the creation of a market economy has depended heavily on foreign capital, mainly foreign direct investment by

Corruption is prevalent as political parties are often controlled by behind-the-scenes economic interests

large multinational companies. Unlike in established Western democracies, domestic capital has played a relatively small role in the new market economy.

If we take into account that market entities, such as small and mid-size businesses, played a crucial role in the creation of civil societies in traditional democracies, the relative absence of this segment of the market economy in post-communist countries has been an obstacle to building vibrant civil societies.

Public space, one of the pillars of modern democracies, is not such a developed principle as it is in established democracies and it may, in fact, never be so. Economic policies dominated the process of democracy-building, with the unfortunate result that the importance of anything "public" diminished. As a result, wherever public space began appearing it quickly came under pressure →

→ from markets and was often colonised by private interests.

The pressure that globalisation puts on the very concept of nation state combines with the traditional Czech distrust of the state to create an explosive mix. In other words, the Czech state is not only under pressure from globalisation but also from a number of traditional prejudices against the state.

Combined with the traditionally strong anti-elitist sentiments in Czech society, which, in turn, come from plebeian traditions and the provincialism of a country that did not have its own political elites for centuries, these are potentially dangerous trends. The jury is still out on the question of whether the Czech post-communist era will in the end be replaced by a fully functioning democracy and a state people trust and with which they identify. ⊠

©Jiri Pehe
www.indexoncensorship.org

Jiri Pehe is director of New York University's centre in Prague. He was director of the political department for former Czech President Vaclav Havel from 1997 to 1999. He co-authored The Prague Spring: A Mixed Legacy (University Press of America)

OF LOVE.

...is a fragrant blossom, that maketh glad th...

POETRY
INTERNATIONAL
THURSDAY 17 – MONDAY 21 JULY 2014

Bold and inspiring festival of poetry, film and spoken word that brings together over 100 internationally renowned poets and artists from all over the world.

EVENTS INCLUDE

Love Each Other Or Perish
50 greatest love poems

***Poetry International* Launch**
Robert Hass, Ana Blandiana, Carolyn Forché, Kutti Revathi, Nikola Madzirov and Mohamed El Deeb

Poetry After Rilke
Sujata Bhatt, Durs Grünbein, Patrick McGuiness, Don Paterson and Karen Leeder

Poetry Society Lecture: The Poet as Eye-Witness
Carolyn Forché

Literary activism: Is poetry the strongest form of protest?

Brecht and Steffin
Love in a time of exile and war

Poetry Film Competition Prize-giving Ceremony

***Poetry International* Finale**
August Kleinzahler, Durs Grünbein, Sujata Bhatt, Don Paterson, Serhiy Zhadan and Bejan Matur

Plus workshops, music, poetry films, translations, new commissions, spoken word, free events and more.

BOOK NOW
SOUTHBANKCENTRE.CO.UK/ POETRYINTERNATIONAL

@litsouthbank
#PoetryInternational

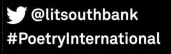

Supported using public funding by
ARTS COUNCIL ENGLAND
LOTTERY FUNDED

FESTIVAL OF LOVE
SOUTHBANK CENTRE

The new divide

43(2): 36/40 | DOI: 10.1177/0306422014537952

The fall of the Berlin Wall created a bigger gap between rich and poor than there was previously in eastern Europe, and discrimination against minorities continues today, argues award-winning German author **Thomas Rothschild**

THESE DAYS FEW would dispute that the Soviet Union was a totalitarian state. And because it was "communist", as its most ardent advocates and its bitterest opponents would declare in splendid harmony, communism became, at least for the critics, the source of all evil. Uttered again and again *ad nauseam* over the decades, this statement has contributed to the idea that capitalism and democracy are somehow two sides of the same coin, as if Pinochet's military dictatorship in Chile and Hitler's National Socialism weren't also forms of capitalism. They certainly weren't shining examples of democracy. Those who stood to profit from capitalism, and had more to lose than chains, had good reason to discredit any alternative. They used every opportunity to reinforce the assumption that the vested interests of the ruling classes are identical to the interests of the general public, for which Karl Marx coined the perhaps rather antiquated, and yet still perfectly functional, term "ideology" or "false consciousness".

Meanwhile, the theory of trickle-down economics has become a deeply ingrained conviction: if you feed your horse enough oats, the sparrows will also get fat on the leftovers. You don't need an example as ghastly as the Soviet Union to dispel any alternative to capitalism from the conscious-

ness of those who have more elementary concerns to worry about than the right to read The New York Times or spend their summers in the Riviera. But anyone who has not completely forgotten the crimes for which we hold the Soviet Union to account will discover that they still linger, albeit in a changed form. Since the demise of what we referred to with the misnomer "communist" or "socialist", the distribution of wealth has changed beyond recognition. The rich today are far richer than the wealthiest party officials ever were, while the poor are also poorer and, more importantly, more numerous than in the worst post-war years of the USSR. Putin is no closer to a flawless democrat than the Tsar was before 1917 or, for that matter, Mikhail Gorbachev, a figure who is idolised by the Germans. Because of reunification, they are more indebted to Gorbachev than his own countrymen are. In other words, the crimes committed in and by the Soviet Union, which simply cannot be glossed over, were not communist crimes; they were Russian.

For Russia lives by the laws of a superpower, even if the country can no longer punch its weight on the international stage in the same way that the Soviet Union did during the Cold War. The USA is also granted certain rights, whether through necessity or

ABOVE: A homeless man sits outside the GUM department store in Moscow, where there is a massive divide between rich and poor

out of conviction, for which smaller states would be condemned – not only morally, but also with sanctions. If the standards that were used to judge Slobodan Milošević were universal, some might argue that Vladimir Putin and George W. Bush would both face trial in The Hague, and perhaps even Gorbachev and Barack Obama. And yet in the countries that a quarter of a century ago shook off Russian colonial rule and ushered in the capitalist economic order, it's certainly not a given that democracy has taken root and flourished, no matter what the investors and developers would have had us believe.

The most glaring example at the moment is Hungary. Seemingly legitimised by democracy because he was elected with a landslide majority, Prime Minister Viktor Orbán has, bit by bit, dismantled pretty much every institution that is generally considered a cornerstone of democracy. Now we have to be careful here. Sadly, the defenders of Orbán's politics are right when they point out that even the supposedly liberal West is not as impeccable as it presents itself to be. Nowhere is party protectionism as pro-

nounced as in the ostensibly democratic Austria. As Austrian newspaper Der Standard recently reported there are significant links in Austria between party membership and top jobs in government-related industries. The first comprehensive study of the relationship, by the University of Vienna, found that about 50 per cent of senior roles in large

An electoral majority can be just as anti-democratic or fascist as a government

companies with a government relationship went to those with party membership. Of course, this comparison does not bolster Hungary's democratic claims, but only confirms Austria's underdeveloped democracy.

But in Hungary the mockery of democracy goes far beyond uninhibited nepotism. At its worst, outsiders criticise nationalist tendencies, including small-minded aggression against travellers, Jews and the homeless, and especially anti-EU propaganda. →

→ Here, too, we have to be careful in our interpretation. Where is the borderline between worrying about threatened minorities and defending what Brussels sees as the interests of individual states and global companies?

Orbán was elected to his office by a majority. That much is not in doubt. And yet a majority is no guarantee of democracy. An electoral majority can be just as anti-democratic or fascist as a government. For some, what is happening in Hungary prompts worrying memories of the Weimar Republic, when state institutions looked on helplessly, or even approvingly, as Nazi troops forced their way in. Fidesz, Orban's ruling conservative party, is not Jobbik, the party of the radical nationalists, but it still woos voters with emotive nationalism. Previously sup-

History is being rewritten in eastern Europe. The glorification of the SS is not a marginal hobby confined to a few isolated nutters

pressed far-right writers who had links with fascism have been introduced into the school curriculum.

With a little imagination, we can understand Orbán's success. There is something alluring about the European dream. Doing away with nation states is a utopia with some appeal, although one can't help but wonder why its proponents are so keen to set the vested interests of Europe against the national interests of the states, instead of setting its sights on the developing world. The reason is, of course, that the EU is, above all, an economic bulwark against the USA, and with time also Russia and China. But precisely because the EU's concerns are chiefly economic, and in particular in the interests of large multinational companies,

and because achieving equal social standards across Europe is far from its driving passion, resentment is quite easy to understand, especially among the population of the smaller member states. The left has made the mistake of leaving it to the right to condemn European bureaucratic centralisation. Add to this the rather unappetising alternatives served up by the social democrats, not only in Hungary but in other eastern European countries, and further west by François Mitterrand, Tony Blair and Gerhard Schröder. And that's before we even consider the corruption cases in which the social democratic parties have been embroiled.

In a sense, the Eurosceptic policies in Hungary echo the campaigns against the hegemony of the German-speaking government in the 19th-century Habsburg Empire. Nationalism, not only in Hungary, was at that time closely associated with democratic demands, where the pursuit of sovereignty within the smaller political unit was by no means reactionary. The jury is still out on whether or not EU economic restraints and interference in the smaller countries' monetary policies actually help consolidate democracy. But, either way, we don't tend to hear much talk of solidarity from Germany, France, Italy or the UK if jobs are scrapped in Croatia, Poland, the Baltic states or Hungary.

So while it's clear to see how Orbán wins the sympathy of his people with his nationalist critique of European meddling, what's less easy to understand is why this desire for independence needs to be associated with jingoism on the domestic stage. It is this, not its foreign policy, that nudges Orbán's Hungary in the direction of a fascist regime.

What's alarming is not the anti-EU stance, but the way the Hungarian government has turned against its own people, discriminating against minorities and dismantling basic democratic rights. In May 2012, the former Austrian Federal Chancellor Wolfgang

Schüssel, of the conservative People's Party, praised his Hungarian counterpart Orbán, expecting that his government would "act fairly when it uses the two-thirds majority it won in parliament."

The renaissance of nationalism, which we can understand to a certain degree, but which we might ordinarily see as an outdated product of the 19th century, linked to the disastrous experiences of the 20th century, is all the more worrying in that it is not limited to Hungary, but is now the most striking common feature uniting the states of the former Soviet empire. In Hungary, monuments are being erected to Hungarian ruler Miklós Horthy, who agreed an alliance with the Nazis. In Poland, there is a proliferation of Piłsudski streets and squares. When you remind the Poles that Józef Piłsudski as head of state didn't put on his kid gloves to deal with the opposition, you feel the full force of their wrath. In Slovakia, the Catholic priest Jozef Tiso, president from 1939 to 1945, who was hanged as a war criminal in 1947, has been honoured with a plaque in Zilinia, and there is a monument in Bauska to the Latvian Waffen SS. Some argue that because the new (who are also the old) national heroes fought against the Soviet Union and communism, some people are burying the memory of their fascist domestic politics and seeking to legitimise collaboration with the Nazis.

History is being rewritten in eastern Europe. The glorification of the SS is not a marginal hobby confined to a few isolated nutters. In 2012, no less a man than the Latvian president, Andris Berzins called upon his countrymen to honour the men of the Waffen SS; they had fought for their country, after all. If Soviet crimes like the Katyn massacre were once whitewashed, manipulated, relativised, now there is a tendency to do the same with crimes against the Soviet Union. But stylising the Soviet construct as the number-one atrocity of the 20th century, as the unrivalled superlative of evil, has the effect, whether intentionally or not, of exonerat-

ing Nazism. Robert Jungk once spoke of the "Napoleonisation of Hitler", a phenomenon that is already well advanced: in Latvia it is not unlikely that you'll find people identifying with Hitler and Nazism as champions against the greater evil, communism.

Not daring to voice the ultimate consequence of this is the same as distinguishing between the heinous crime that was Nazism and other manifestations of fascism, justifying them on grounds of defending national sovereignty. The unabashed claims now being made in eastern Europe about Piłsudski or Horthy are the sort of things we will perhaps soon hear in Italy about Mussolini, in Austria about Englebert Dollfuss and in Spain about Francisco Franco. It's a red line that still hasn't quite

Twenty-five years after the fall of the Iron Curtain, the world, if we're honest, is no better

been crossed; the portrait of the Austrofascist Dollfuss is still tucked away in the Austrian Christian Democrats (ÖVP) faction's room in the parliament building, perhaps out of shame, or more likely out of deference to their coalition partner, the Social Democrats. But why shouldn't an Austrian president follow the footsteps of his Latvian colleague? Why should he not seek to reinstate Dollfuss's honour in the plenary hall of the parliament? He did fight for his country, after all, and unlike the Latvian Waffen SS troops, he was actually murdered by the Nazis. And yet he was also a fascist.

Twenty-five years after the fall of the Iron Curtain, the world, if we're honest, is no better. The threat of war has not been reduced; it has merely shifted geographically. The military conflicts in the Gulf, Afghanistan or the former Yugoslavia saw no respite with the end of the Cold War; →

→ the Middle East is still the same powder keg that it was before; and now there is the Crimea. If you point out that the Serbs and the Croats, the Slovenes and the Bosnians, the Montenegrins and Macedonians actually lived together relatively peacefully in Tito's Yugoslavia, if you remind people that in the GDR there was no threat to foreigners from neo-Nazis, you generally hear the counter argument that these controversies were always simmering under the surface, but were only held in check by the police state. That may be so. But for those affected, it surely makes a considerable difference whether a feud is latent, or whether it is explosive and bloody. An asylum seeker whose temporary accommodation has been the target of an arson attack or a woman who has been raped and had her village overrun by marauding mobs might perhaps see the monitoring of phone lines by the state as a comparatively minor evil. Especially since the Edward Snowden and NSA affair has reminded us recently that the Stasi weren't alone in dabbling in this little pastime. Again, not everything we find distasteful can be ascribed to one particular ideology.

Since the fall of the Berlin Wall, eastern Europe has certainly enjoyed some of the blessings of capitalism – freedom of movement and a wider range of consumer goods – but it has also witnessed a growing gap between rich and poor that never existed before. Even when it comes to freedom of expression, on which the West prides itself, we have started to hesitate. Orbán has demonstrated that this freedom can indeed be effectively restrained even under the conditions of capitalism. Granted, one no longer faces jail for speaking out against the state, but you could certainly lose your job. And a certain former Austrian chancellor is perfectly happy with that.

And what of the minorities? Their protection at least is as much a criterion for democracy as is the respect for the major-ity. Have they benefitted from the fall of the wall? The Vietnamese or Africans, who no longer dare to go out in the evening in the "nationally liberated zones" of east Germany? The Roma, who are either trapped in ghettos or deported? The homosexuals who face legally sanctioned harassment in Russia? They are unlikely to feel moved by the rhetoric on the anniversary of the fall of the wall. ☒

Translated by Ruth Ahmedzai Kemp

© Thomas Rothschild
www.indexoncensorship.org

Thomas Rothschild taught literary studies at Stuttgart University. He writes for several publications in Germany and Austria. He was awarded the Bruno Kreisky prize for political books in 1997 and the Austrian state prize for literary criticism in 1992

The other wall

43(2): 41/47 | DOI: 10.1177/0306422014534799

When the Berlin Wall came down, certain divides remained. But Europe's dividing line has now shifted east, says **Irena Maryniak**

AS CROWDS SURGED through the checkpoints between East and West Berlin on 9 November 1989, and people danced on the wall or hacked away chunks of concrete to take home, it seemed that collectivist ideology had crumbled in the Soviet Union and eastern Europe. Individualism, and of course capitalism, had triumphed. Yet when the wall fell, the ideological and political rift it symbolised did not close. Instead it shifted and became a philosophical, cultural and emotional disconnect, functioning rather like a shutter along the eastern border of the Baltic states, down the western border of Belarus, and appearing (in varying guises and at different times) in regions of Ukraine or Moldova.

East of this more permeable barrier, communism may have been relegated to history, just as it was further west, but the perception remained that the social-collective shapes, indeed owns, people; that individuals must conform; and that, ultimately, the integrity and cohesion of the group are paramount. But the myths, lore and beliefs that help to cement states and national groups are not the same everywhere in the region – far from it. There are starkly conflicting sensibilities, for example, about the myth of medieval Kievan Rus (a state that covered large areas of present day Ukraine, Belarus and western Russia until the 13th century). Irrespective of historical perceptions and loyalties, however, in eastern parts of Europe feelings of group integrity and mission stand in stark contrast to the Western liberal sense that as individuals, within the framework of democratic consent, we possess and can invent ourselves.

Over the past decade or so in Russia the Kremlin has enlisted the Russian religious tradition, alongside other storylines, to encourage state cohesion and the priority of group goals over individual ambitions. The canonisation of Tsar Nicholas II (murdered by the Bolsheviks); memories of imperial glory; wartime struggles against Nazi Germany; a nostalgia for global power and the mellow togetherness of life in the USSR; Nikita Khrushchev's "mistake" in giving Ukraine to Crimea in 1954 – all have been co-opted into the campaign. But underlying these narratives is a deeper cultural predisposition to communality and collectivism: a sense that the human personality and the group which defines it are somehow destined to fuse. According to the Orthodox Christian tradition still prevalent in Russia, human fulfilment and salvation rest in a merger between self, community and – at the religious level that underpins all this – deity. In this cultural context the Western political principles of opposition, bargaining, pressure and conflict between competing groups are bound to be anathema.

Eastern and central European countries, once under Imperial or Soviet Russian rule, uphold their own communitarian traditions. But with weak, historically unstable →

ABOVE: Anti-government protesters carry a Ukrainian flag while driving through Independence Square, Kiev, in February

Credit: Vasily Fedosenko/Reuters

→ boundaries they are also in-between spaces where margins are smudged, cultures cross and opposing ideas clash. Demarcation is hazy ("senseless", the exiled Czech writer Milan Kundera once said) because it has been so often disputed. The plains of eastern middle Europe make the perfect battlefield. Today, Ukraine's cultural, linguistic and religious fault lines are widely known. The western Ukrainian city of Lviv was previously named Lemberg, or Lwów, or Lvov, depending on whether the administration was Austro-Hungarian, Polish or Russian. Beyond Ukraine, the east European experi-

ence as a whole is grounded in memories of changing borders, mutating roles and identities. Yet borderlands are more than just peripheries. They are centres of national identity and reinvention that reflect local needs and external geopolitical pressures. A hundred years ago a shooting in one such borderland ignited cross-European conflict.

"For us Europe is emotion, not rules," the Ukrainian philosopher Volodymyr Yermolenko wrote recently. "It is a far-off ideal, in which we have faith. Europe is a deity with whom we wish to unite." Yermolenko's words connect painfully, perhaps reluctantly, with that time-honoured east European consensus between individual and community, and between the community and some kind of masterminding power.

Pre-revolutionary Russian society was largely sustained by the myth of its identity as a "right thinking" nation. The word *pravoslavie* (Russian Orthodox Christianity), also means "right worship" or "right belief". At the turn of the 20th century it was common for a rural Russian to identify himself simply as *pravoslavny*, one who is theologically "right". This kind of prescriptive and collectivist thinking – which once made Marxism so palatable in the Russian context – has led anti-Soviet dissidents, as much as communist party functionaries and post-Soviet bureaucrats, to share a horror of Western political ideals like pluralism, individualism or tolerance. "If diversity becomes the highest principle there can be no universal human values," the Soviet dissident writer Alexander Solzhenitsyn thundered in 1985. "If there is no right or wrong what restraints remain? If there is no universal basis for it there can be no morality."

Vladimir Putin's vision of a cohesive, hierarchical, supra-national United Russia is a direct politicised extension of this rationale. Eastern Christianity acknowledges that boundaries are elusive. "Right belief" has no geographical limits, it is consensual and universal. Russian culture by its nature impinges on ideas about unifying humanity. The 19th-century novelist Fyodor Dostoyevsky (avidly studied in Russia) believed his country had a unique mission in the world: "To become a true Russian ... is ... to become if you like universal man", he wrote.

Today, Vladislav Surkov, the Kremlin's chief apologist for authoritarian state capitalism, would probably agree. He has spoken of the Russian "aspiration to political wholeness" and "idealisation of goals" and is happy to blend religious idiom with Hegelian and New Age ideas. "Russian conscious-ness is clearly holistic [and] intuitive and opposed to [the] mechanistic [and] reductionist," he has said. "Synthesis prevails over analysis, idealism over pragmatism, images over logic, intuition over reasoning, general over particular." His remark: "Culture is fate. God made us Russian. Citizens of Russia" has been widely quoted.

West of that post-Berlin Wall gap between communitarian sensibilities and neo-liberal individualism, we prefer to think of morality in terms of personal choice, will and consent. The philosopher Michael Sandel has termed this the "voluntarist conception", which implies that we are independent agents, free to choose, unbound by moral ties or collective responsibility. Within the Western framework of the rule of law, separation of

The Kremlin's policy and propaganda are reflecting a similar reverence for state power, hardening the virtual walls and disconnects criss-crossing eastern Europe

powers, independent media and fair elections, we cling to the thought that we possess our lives and ourselves.

The crumbling of "solidaristic" values in post-wall Poland seems to confirm the unassailable potency of this position. The astonishing social cohesion the country demonstrated in the 1980s proved specific to its times. Once feelings of liberty and independence prevailed, the moral unit represented by the Solidarity trade union (once 10 million strong) fragmented. The bond that had held it – *oni*, "they", those godless communists – had melted away. In a neo-liberal context with a free market and few economic or social constraints, people felt apprehensive and threatened by those they had previously trusted. Workers sensed that the intellectuals →

ABOVE: Vladimir Putin with Russian Orthodox Bishop Patriarch Kirill

→ with whom they had been allied with in the 1980s were no longer committed to their interests – and they were right.

Solidarity had fought for values rather than labour contracts or working conditions. Its language had been elevated, with a moral, anti-discursive undertone. The emphasis was on asserting independence though unity. After 1989, people who had been partners in political resistance became competitors for jobs, money and prestige. Solidarity's membership plummeted. A movement that had struggled and negotiated peacefully for participation in Western libertarianism and the free market, disintegrated in rows and

recrimination. Speaking out in an organised way through interest associations was a skill few either had or wanted. Perhaps negotiating over wages or hours seemed insipid or trite in the wake of an ideological revolution.

"Culture is fate," the voice of the Kremlin, Vladislav Surkov, has said. Yet how curious that, in 1984, the writer Milan Kundera used language very similar to Surkov's to convey an entirely different allegiance. In an article entitled The Tragedy of Central Europe, which argued that Soviet satellite countries had been "stolen" from western Europe, he wrote: "Central Europe is not a state: it is culture or fate".

What do these unlikely echoes from different ends of the east European political spectrum tell us? That you cannot choose where you are born? That central Europeans and Russians, despite their differences, share a common, deterministic streak? Or that these diametrically opposed figures – Kundera, originally from Czechoslovakia, and Surkov from Russia – share an underlying assumption that the community into which you merge, its way of expressing itself, its collective memory and its identity defines who you are, along with your loyalties and responsibilities. Communitarian sensibilities run deep. For central Europeans, Kundera explained in his article, "the word Europe is not a geographical but a spiritual notion". For a country that "feels" European, to be excluded from Europe is to be "driven from its own destiny, beyond its own history", he continued. "It loses the essence of its identity." Three decades on, Volodymyr Yermolenko has observed that for people in the countries of the former Soviet Bloc: "Europe is still a vision, an ideal, a utopia…a kind of mystical ecstasy."

To Westerners in the digital age, high-flown language of this kind can seem poignant but passé. Like the word "solidarity", it resonates with images of striking Gdansk shipyard workers on their knees in prayer. But in a letter to the Polish journal Respublica Nowa published in February, a demonstrator in Kiev's Independence Square, Aleksandra Kovaleva, expressed some of the ambivalence felt in Ukraine towards the West's perceived lack of "solidaristic" ideals. "I can't imagine a Europe in which people would be capable of fighting and dying for freedom and dignity," Kovaleva wrote bitterly. "These concepts seem to have little relevance for a sleepy and well-fed Europe."

Closer to the former imperial centre, group identity is increasingly firmly consolidated. Over the past decade, Russia has been defining itself in anti-European terms. According to the Sociological Institute of the Russian Academy of Sciences, over a third of Russians share the view that theirs "is a unique Eurasian civilisation", marked out in contrast to a West that is grasping, meddling, immoral and sexually deviant. The Kremlin has denounced the hypocrisy of Western condemnation of "spheres of influence" in Europe, given the incorporation of the Baltic states, Poland and other former communist countries into NATO and the EU. Cold War-style rhetoric transmitted via Russian television to Ukraine or Belarus has played on deep-rooted anxieties about Western infiltration, as well as public suspicion of outsiders, gays or other degenerates with little respect for sacrosanct values. Gender boundaries have come to express the cultural conflict between social conservatives and social liberals. State-controlled Russian media like to suggest that, in the West, the gay lobby has made inroads into the corridors of powers. A programme screened on a major TV channel, the Repressive Minority, in June last year discussed "gay totalitarianism", for example. A December headline in Komsomolskaya Pravda read: "Gay fuel in the Maidan fire: Ukraine called to join Europe by nationalists, anti-semites, neo-Nazis and homosexuals".

Russia's leadership is branding itself as a global moral authority transcending borders, nations and continents. In his State of the Nation speech in December, Vladimir Putin promised that Russia would lead in defending traditional, conservative principles against a stream of global "anti-democratic" propaganda calling on people "to accept without question the equality of good and evil". Putin subsequently gained expressions of approval from erstwhile Republican presidential nominee and editor of The American Conservative, Pat Buchanan, who praised his moral clarity and asked: "Is Putin one of us?"

All this seems a far cry from the days of the socialist collective, but the paradoxes associated with divisions between individualism and collectivism, selves and others, inner and outer, often form a blurred picture. As group-focused ideology disintegrated in

After 1989, people who had been partners in political resistance became competitors for jobs, money and prestige

the 1980s, it was harmonised action and group solidarity that finally opened the Berlin Wall. Meanwhile in Moscow – a society still commanded by Marxist-Leninist ideology – informal organisations were multiplying, unofficial publishing flourished, and literature authorised by the censor hinted at probing, subversive and sometimes wacky ideas. Soviet atheism and religious repression animated a fascination with myth and spirituality, which later helped bring such influence and prestige to the Russian Orthodox Church. In 1987, the writer Tatyana Tolstaya – then at the start of what became an international writing career – remarked, exasperated, that Muscovites were "totally absorbed in saving their own soul".

This was the age of *glasnost* or "openness". But amid calls for an end to public disinformation, revelations about conditions →

→ in labour camps, dismay about historical atrocities, enthusiasm for New Age ideas, and discussion about setting the world to rights, the Moscow "intelligentsia" were also showing unease about the growing power of a group of litterateurs with neo-Stalinist sympathies. The nationalist critic Pyotr Palievsky – then director of the Institute of World Literature and widely viewed as a member of this controlling group – once told me that there was conflict between "a revolutionary desire to assert oneself over Nature, and the religious urge to submit its wisdom". But, he added firmly, one thing Soviet writers would never do was promote individualism, classical liberalism or democracy. Meanwhile, among more liberal Soviet critics, there was concern about a new political project linked with the neo-Stalinist group: not communism or

The walls around the elites isolate them from the majority, stoking feelings of rage

socialism but "etatism", which Irina Rodnanskaya, then senior editor at the journal Novyi Mir called "a religious adulation of the state".

A generation on, the Kremlin's policy and propaganda are reflecting a similar reverence for state power, hardening the virtual walls and disconnects criss-crossing eastern Europe and reaching way beyond. Within the region there are numerous divides: linguistic, cultural, religious, moral, economic, historical and philosophical. Equally, digital connectivity has provided "resonance chambers" for group feeling, and created decentralised communication patterns that can be used to embarrass the authorities and assemble crowds. But, unlike the panels of reinforced concrete that split Berlin between 1961 and 1989, until recently the barriers seemed flexible and permeable. How far will they now freeze?

And then there is that other, glaring gap: the social and economic fault-line between elites and voters, which seems the least penetrable barrier of all. Inequality colours our social perception, Richard Wilkinson and Kate Pickett have argued in The Spirit Level. Feelings of superiority and inferiority, dominance and subordination take over and shape our social relationships. In eastern Europe civic activism remains a dangerous job, and the organised expression of group interests is undeveloped. The walls that enclose elites holding funds stashed away in tax havens abroad, and isolate them from the majority, continue to stoke up feelings of untold rage.

The Russian information space has been filled with news about the activities of neo-Nazis and extreme nationalists in Ukraine. Yet the Independence Square protests in Kiev were very largely simply about justice. They expressed a desire to break out of the stifling, clannish, top-down system which, as the Ukrainian commentator Mykola Riabchuk has pointed out, "destroyed the court system, accumulated enormous reserves via corruption schemes and encroached heavily on human rights and civil liberties". These days Ukrainians are likely to be yearning less for union with European cultural values than for regulation, rule of law, checks on power and a free-trade zone.

The problem is that the Kremlin's arguments about historical bonds and the West's disregard for Moscow's status or interests cover up a basic contradiction. The solidaristic narrative of shared memory and emotion, loyalty and biding with your own, is shielding a hierarchical form of rule, which holds that once you are at the top you are accountable only to your personal will, beliefs or fantasies, not to voters or any notion of the inalienable human right to life and liberty. In other words if you have links high enough up the chain of command, you can enjoy entitlement and impunity, an array of life choices, as well as that lavish lifestyle in Zermatt or the Côte d'Azur. More importantly, as the Russian political columnist Kirill Rogov wrote recently, this kind of power structure also implies that in practice "the right to use force takes priority over the rights of citizens". All of which makes the proclaimed communalist narrative – with its 19th-century take on Russian exclusivity and mission – look much like hollow rhetoric if not some kind of diversionary tactic. East of the new "wall", do people need that old Slavophile story to live by? ☒

© Irena Maryniak
www.indexoncensorship.org

Irena Maryniak is the author of Spirit of the Totem: Religion and Myth in Soviet Fiction 1964-1988, and Offence: The Christian Case

The mystery of regional identity

43(2): 48/52 | DOI: 10.1177/0306422014535880

Has German crime fiction reflected a unified national culture post 1989? **Regula Venske** tries to detect a trend

YOU MIGHT BE familiar with such German exports into English as *Blitzkrieg* or *Schadenfreude*. Here's a new one: *Krimi*. It's our slightly pejorative nickname for a crime novel – which we apply particularly to German crime novels.

Of course, we do have a more serious-sounding compound for the thing: *Kriminalroman*, crime novel. And there are some strange German writers who insist they don't write *Krimis* but crime novels – or even novels. But every German crime writer who has done a reading in a small-town library or town hall, with wine being served and music to accompany the event, is sure to have heard a version of a pop song which was number three in German charts in the autumn of 1962: Ohne Krimi geht die Mimi nie ins Bett, which tells the story of a woman named Mimi who never goes to bed without reading a crime novel – while her husband desperately urges her to switch off the light.

What does German *Krimi* – and, to be even more specific, the booming subgenre called *Regional-Krimi* – have to do with German identity, our inferiority complexes, the unification of east and west and possibly even German notions of blood and soil, or, to put it more mildly, the longing for one's home and place of origin?

German crime writing – both east and west – became respectable only in the 1970s. West German crime writers of that generation would often name the Swedish journalists Maj Sjöwall and Per Wahlöö, best known as the husband-and-wife team who wrote the Martin Beck series of crime thrillers, as models for their writing. Like them they wanted to criticise problems in society, so this type of crime writing was labelled *Soziokrimi*. Friedrich Schiller's 1786 story Der Verbrecher aus verlorener Ehre (The Criminal who Lost his Honour) would have fallen into this category – if it hadn't been labelled "classic" already, and if anybody had cared to remember.

One of the writers who wrote fine *Soziokrimis* in the 1970s was Richard Hey, whose last name is pronounced like "Hi", rhyming with "die", but whose name we younger kids pronounced as a native speaker of English would pronounce Hey (rhyming with May), automatically assuming either he was English or American by origin, or that he was using an English pseudonym, since serious German crime writing didn't really exist. It was only in 1997, when Hey was to be awarded an honorary Glauser award for his lifetime achievement and I was asked to deliver an encomium, that I learned his →

ABOVE: Germany's crime novels suggest the country's national identity is still fractured

→ name was originally German and that I should pronounce it the German way.

Around 1980, the Heyne publishing house made a daring attempt to move crime fiction up-market, placing a stamp on the covers of its Blue Series pocketbooks saying "*Deutscher Autor*" (German writer). The stamp had a peculiar resemblance to those stamps that every West German housewife was well familiar with, *Deutsche Marken-butter (*German butter). The Goldmann publishing house followed by creating a special imprint to republish classic crime by German writers, Sammlung deutscher Kriminalautoren (German Crime Writers' Collection). There was more confidence, and money, in German crime writing than ever before.

After the collapse of the wall, highbrow critics started a search for the "novel of reunification"

Richard Hey was one of the first Germans – if not the first – to have a policewoman investigate his cases. But when, at the end of the 1980s, a new subgenre emerged, *Frauenkrimi*, crime fiction starring a female investigator, written by a female writer or directed at female readers – the term never really was defined – not many would have remembered Hey's marvellous policewoman-protagonist, Katharina Ledermacher, with her tiny red high heels. The writers who then appeared on the scene usually named as role models either Sjöwall and Wahlöö or American writers such as Sara Paretsky and Sue Grafton and their "tough cookies" invading a supposedly male genre. By coincidence, the *Frauenkrimi* subgenre emerged around the time when the wall collapsed. Names to be mentioned here are Pieke Biermann, whose debut novel Potsdamer Ableben (Potsdam Death) was

first published in 1987, Sabine Deitmer (Bye, Bye Bruno) and Doris Gercke (Weinschröter, du mußt hängen, Weinschröter, You Must Hang).

There was crime writing in East Germany, too. The imprint DIE, short for Delikte, Indizien, Ermittlungen – Offences, Evidence, Investigations – was started in 1970 at Das Neue Berlin publishing house. By 1989, it had published 130 crime novels by such writers as Fritz Erpenbek and Tom Wittgen (pseudonym for Ingeburg Siebenstädt). There were certain no-go areas for East German crime: you couldn't have a bad cop, and there had to be a clear moral to the story. But East German writers undoubtedly did a fine job walking the tightrope between ideology and censorship. Their writings demonstrated a subtlety that West Germans did not have to develop.

After the collapse of the wall, highbrow critics started a search for the "novel of reunification", the novel which would depict the so-called *Wende*, the fall of the wall. They ignored the fact that crime writers such as Dagmar Scharsich (Die gefrorene Charlotte, Frozen Charlotte, 1993) and Hartmut Mechtel (Der unsichtbare Zweite, The Invisible Second Man), 1996, were dealing with recent German history and writing what you might have called *Wende-Krimis*, crime novels about the fall of the wall.

In 1992, my then-publisher Michael Kellner took part in a panel discussion on German crime literature and came up with a challenging statement. Crime novels, he said, are the modern form of what is called *Heimatroman* in German, a sentimental and nostalgic – if not reactionary – genre set against a local background, your *Heimat* (homeland), the place you feel you belong. *Heimat* does not necessarily have to refer to your home country: it is more about the region, the landscape, its taste and smells and the people it shapes, their culture, their dialect. The *Heimatroman* was a genre associated with rural areas – particularly the Alps and the Black Forest. But *Krimi,* said Kellner, can be considered a form of *Heimatroman* situated in big cities. Kellner published *Hamburg-Krimis,* crime novels set in Hamburg, which kept the highbrow literature part of his small independent publishing house going for a while.

Today the *Regionalkrimi* subgenre – crime novels set in a certain region – is going strong. Although crime writing originated as an urban genre, there is not a single region left in Germany that hasn't been covered by *Krimi. Allgäu-Krimi, Ostfriesland-Krimi, Münster-Krimi, Ostsee-Krimi, Nordsee-Krimi, Taunuskrimi* … you might get the impression that reunited Germany is being split up into little states, kingdoms, dukedoms and tribal regions as it was pre-1871. There are not so many *Regionalkrimis* set in former East Germany, and there are not so many set in regions that are not popular tourist destinations – though there are examples of regions becoming popular with tourists because of crime novels set in them. The prime example is the Eifel region, on the borders of Germany, Belgium and Luxemburg. Former journalist and war correspondent Michael Preute published his first *Eifelkrimi,* Eifelblues, in 1989, choosing for a pseudonym the name of the place in the region to which he had moved, Berndorf. Each new title – Eifelgold, Eifelconnection, Eifelkrieg – sells some 150,000 copies in the first three months, making Jacques Berndorf, the "father of *Regionalkrimi*", the best-selling German crime writer.

The German addiction to *Regionalkrimi* does not have much to do with literature, says critic Thomas Wörtche, who uses the term *Krimi* only in a derogatory sense. "It has to do with Germans' self-reflection and self-consciousness. They want easy reading, and they want to avoid the accusation that they idealise their *Heimat* too much. So they seek refuge in a totally superfluous and irrelevant crime plot. Even the least talented amateur can feel part of a discourse."

There is also a boom of Scandinavian, particularly Swedish, crime fiction in Germany, and this may stem from the very same nostalgic feelings. Many of the Swedish crime novels convey the cosiness of Miss Marple's village (a similar culture of everyone knowing everyone's business), while at the same time dealing with challenges faced by all modern Western societies: illegal trading of weapons and women, drugs, problems of migration and integration, the rise of right-wing nationalism and international terrorism. But the Swedes have two things Germans lack: a capital that they all accept as their capital and a landscape that everybody recognises as Swedish, be it the sea, the islands, the woods or the lakes. In Germany, however, a Bavarian is not very likely to identify with

You might get the impression that reunited Germany is being split up into little states, kingdoms, dukedoms and tribal regions as it was pre-1871

Berlin and "the Prussians", and many west Germans have spent more holidays in Italy, France or Spain – or Thailand or Florida – than anywhere further east in Germany. *Regionalkrimis* seem to offer reassurance in rough times. There may be some irony in the fact that at the very same moment when our neighbours feared the rise of a Great Unified Germany after 1989, Germans themselves retreated to a somewhat more moderate form of patriotism, identifying with their regional background instead and thus asserting themselves as Bavarians, Saxons, or even Hamburgians, rather than feeling "German". Sometimes, one might think we still had a fragmented view of ourselves as if the unification of 1871 had not quite taken place yet.

There is a highly popular TV-format that has been broadcast by National German →

→ Broadcasting (ARD, formerly West Germany) for more than 40 years now, called Tatort (scene of crime). It is the longest-running and most popular TV-format ever. Here, due to the federal system of German public broadcasting, you have teams investigating in practically every region in Germany, namely 20 different places at the moment. On Sunday nights, when the new Tatort-production comes on, the nation gathers in front of the TV as if it's a secularised church service. As critic Tilman Krause recently pointed out, the Tatort series is all about German work ethics, and it is no coincidence it's broadcast at the end of the weekend, preparing the audience for yet another week of duty and work. According to Krause, even the most beautiful German cities, Hamburg and Munich, are portrayed only by their ugly parts, and the country seems to be unified in a lack of any capacity for enjoyment (good food, for example) and by what he calls a specifically German culture of depression.

So far, we have had *Deutscher Krimi*, *Soziokrimi*, *Frauenkrimi*, and *Regionalkrimi*, all within a few decades. What will come next? Johann Wolfgang von Goethe, our other great classical writer, Schiller's great competitor, used to speak of *Weltliteratur*. One world, one literature, no national boundaries – let alone petty regional labels. This, along with Schiller's free spirit – "Sire, do grant freedom of thought", the famous lines uttered in his drama Don Carlos, Infant of Spain (1787) – would be my dream. ☒

©Regula Venske
www.indexoncensorship.org

Regula Venske is a German writer and general secretary of PEN Germany. Her first crime novel, a parody of both hardboiled male crime fiction as well as *Frauenkrimi*, was first published in 1991. She won the Deutscher Krimi Preis in 1996

Empire line

43(2): 53/55 | DOI: 10.1177/0306422014535882

Long-time Moscow resident **Helen Womack** fears a new Cold War, and sees Russia retreating behind a mental wall of its own making

YURI ANDROPOV, WHO headed the KGB and briefly held Kremlin power in pre-Gorbachev days, believed the Soviet Union could be preserved if its citizens were allowed to travel. Vladimir Putin has made this model work. Depending on their incomes, Russians can now have anything from a package holiday in Turkey to a globe-trotting lifestyle, while Russia itself increasingly resembles the old USSR.

That communist-era joke about a watermelon seller, with only one watermelon to sell – "Well, there's only one Brezhnev but we elect him, don't we?" – is still apt today, when Russians fully expect that Putin will be president for life. They may not be thrilled at the prospect but most will give no more than a fatalistic shrug of the shoulders.

What outsiders must understand is that most Russians, on balance, prefer Putin. The turbulent 1990s were too scary for them. They have traded freedom for shopping, gradually improving living standards and stability. As in Soviet times, those who disagree and crave oxygen are a minority. Only a few will stand up and be counted.

If consumerism stops being a powerful enough new opium for the masses, Putin has shown that he will try imperial adventures and the people are ready to swallow that too. In the parliamentary "debate" on the annexation of Crimea, only one deputy,

Ilya Ponomaryov, risked being called a "fifth columnist" and "traitor" and voted against.

In Putin's Russia, what matters is loyalty, not talent. If you don't conform but think in a different way, you are isolated. If, like my friend L, you happen not only to question the government's policies but also to be gay, you are very isolated indeed.

The deal that Putin long ago made with society is "make money, travel, do what you like but don't rock the political boat". If you don't like it, you can always emigrate." Those who have challenged Putin have found themselves in jail. Anna Politkovskaya is only the most famous of two dozen journalists killed in Russia since 2000 for trying to expose abuses.

The rule of law simply doesn't extend to Russia; expect anything from the justice system, except justice. Non-governmental organisations are regarded with suspicion and squeezed. Independent media have all but been wiped out.

Thinking Russians in big cities can hear a variety of voices by surfing the internet or listening to Echo of Moscow radio, which the authorities allow so the intelligentsia can let off steam. But most Russians get their news and views from Channel One television and that is enough for them.

Unlike the Germans, who confronted their past, the Russians haven't begun to →

ABOVE: People walk past television sets in a shop window during Russian president Vladimir Putin's live nationwide phone-in. Putin said Russia would not seek to cut itself off from the outside world with a Soviet-style Iron Curtain

→ consider their history. Stalin made a few "mistakes" but he won the war, didn't he? Few Russians are aware of how other countries were affected from 1939 to 1945; that Stalin and Hitler had a pact before they fell out. And with the single history book that Putin has ordered for schools, they are not about to be enlightened any time soon.

"We're back to the old ways of teaching our children to lie," said my friend T, a cautious Putin critic, who at home will tell her children one thing while making sure they don't repeat it at school.

What has happened to the Russian soul? The mass of ordinary Russians have sold it. They know this and deep down they feel ashamed. But what can they do? Change is so difficult. "Democracy is not for us," they say, a little wistfully. "We need a strong hand."

Corruption is everywhere, from the top to the bottom of the system. A poorly paid state sector worker will take his boss a small bottle of Cognac in the hope of being included in the payout of New Year bonuses. There's a price for everything, from getting off a criminal charge to saving your son from army conscription or receiving decent medical treatment.

Corruption persists because, nasty as it is, it basically suits everybody. Citizens break the law, knowing that most of the time they will get away with it, while the powers-that-be always have a hook to catch you, if they want to.

In this climate, small businesses struggle. Prime Minister Dmitry Medvedev recently lamented that too many Russian students were choosing careers in the well-padded bureaucracy rather than in the risky world of business. Is it any wonder? The Russian economy remains dependent, as it was in Soviet times, on the export of oil and gas.

So has travel, which supposedly broadens the mind, changed nothing? Not entirely.

It is refreshing to see Russians travelling – travelling anywhere, just the shortest, cheapest foreign trip will do – and coming to the conclusion that their country is neither better nor worse than other countries but simply part of the planet. These people often bring back self-respect and a whiff of freedom, along with the souvenirs in their suitcases.

But others, despite, or perhaps because of, travelling, come back with their inferiority-superiority complexes reinforced. They go to the West and miss the point. They return, saying that Russia has a "special way", as if there is any other way but the way of common humanity. They perceive slights and go so far as to say that Western people hate them.

Often the problem is that Russians are not fluent in English or any other foreign language. Andropov was no fool. A retired KGB officer who told me of Andropov's idea to save the USSR said he knew most Russians would come home because of their need to speak their own language.

Twenty five years after the fall of the Berlin Wall, Germany and the countries of the former Warsaw Pact have clearly benefitted. But Russia is retreating behind a mental wall of its own making. For someone like me, who devoted a whole career to promoting

Unlike the Germans, who confronted their past, the Russians haven't begun to consider their history

East-West understanding, the new Cold War that seems to be approaching is a matter for deep sadness. ⊠

©Helen Womack
www.indexoncensorship.org

Helen Womack has reported from Moscow since 1985. She currently works in Russia for The Sydney Morning Herald. Her book The Ice Walk: Surviving the Soviet Break-up and the New Russia was published last year by Melrose Books

Global View

||||||||||||||||||||||||||||||||||||||||||||||||||||||||||||||||||||||||||||||||||||||||||||||||||||||

43(2): 56/58 | DOI: 10.1177/0306422014537191

Index on Censorship's new CEO, **Jodie Ginsberg**, launches her first column with a look at how fighting online censorship is only one step in an ongoing worldwide battle

THERE IS A moment in cult 2005 film Serenity where the character Mr Universe – a tech geek and hacker who spends his waking hours burrowing into the galaxy's myriad communications systems – is asked to trace an obscure government message being transmitted subliminally. "You can do that?" one of the other characters asks him. "Can't stop the signal…" he replies.

I was reminded of "can't stop the signal" earlier this year when Turkish President Recep Tayyip Erdoğan tried to ban Twitter. "Twitter, schmitter!" Erdoğan told supporters during a fiery rally speech. "I don't care what the international community says. Everyone will witness the power of the Turkish Republic."

The power of the Turkish Republic – or at least the tech-savvy and social media-using part of the republic – was to find workarounds to the ban almost immediately. Twitter itself quickly provided instructions on how to tweet using SMS; users were still able to post by changing their DNS settings or by using Virtual Private Networks. And, most interestingly, these tricks moved rapidly from the online world to the more traditional form of street information-passing: graffiti was scrawled across buildings in Turkey, giving instructions about the internet settings that would circumvent the ban.

For me it was this move, from click to brick, that captured most powerfully the futility of governments' attempts to "stop the signal" in the digital age – and the way in which digital freedom of expression can help free expression in general to flourish. At Index, we are working with colleagues in Europe, as well as in Kenya, Tunisia, Senegal and India to develop tools that enable journalists, writers, artists, and activists to report from their laptop, smartphone, tablets and via SMS on instances of censorship. This will help us to "grow the signal" so we can build a much more detailed picture of the everyday threats to free expression faced globally.

But we would be wrong to think that these tools alone, or the ease with which social media users circumvented and mocked Erdoğan's Twitter ban, means that the battle for freedom of expression is won. Far from it. For while it is not possible to stop the signal, it is possible to stop the signallers.

Take China, for example. Free Weibo, a group shortlisted in Index on Censorship's Freedom of Expression Awards 2014, is doing a remarkable job in republishing all the stories that government censors cut from social media. This helps to keep public discourse alive digitally, but as long as public protest remains outlawed in China and individual dissenters under threat of harassment and arrest, freedom of expression will remain

ABOVE: Journalists on trial on charges of supporting terrorists and spreading false information, in Cairo, Egypt, March 2014

severely curtailed. In Turkey, journalists are regularly jailed by Erdoğan's government or have criminal prosecutions launched against them. Turkish writer and playwright Meltem Arikan, another Index award nominee, fled her homeland after the government accused her of fomenting unrest through her play Mi Minor. Ironically, politicians urged the public to set up Twitter accounts to denounce Arikan for the play.

Every day, free expression in the digital world is being translated into repression in the physical. In countries across the world, journalists, activists, even individuals making throwaway jokes on social media, are being censured, detained and even tortured and killed. In 2013, more than 70 journalists were

Graffiti was scrawled across buildings in Turkey, with instructions on how to circumvent the Twitter ban

killed, two-thirds of those covering political stories. On this year's World Press Freedom Day in early May, Al Jazeera journalists →

→ detained in Egypt for simply doing their jobs learned that they would yet again be denied bail. And this in a country that seemed ,during the Arab Spring, to herald the democratic opportunities afforded to society by technology and social media.

John Naughton, professor of the public understanding of technology at the Open University, wrote at the time of Erdoğan's Twitter ban that the Turkish president had become a laughing stock in less than a week. But, as Naughton also rightly noted in the same article for The Guardian, we laugh at those who strive to stop the signal at our peril. Erdoğan and his like have not lost the free speech battle, nor has the signal yet won. We should not be lulled into thinking that censorship has diminished simply because Twitter workarounds can be found. The persistence of the signal should rather be taken as a rallying call for increased vigilance over all threats to freedom of expression and remind us of the need to defend an individual's right to free expression in all spheres – on stage, outside parliament, in print as well as online. ⊠

© Jodie Ginsberg
www.indexoncensorship.org

Jodie Ginsberg joined Index on Censorship as the new CEO in May

New Books from the Middle East

www.bqfp.com.qa

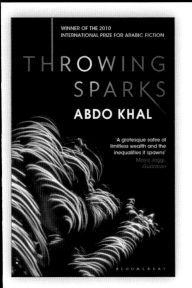

THROWING SPARKS

by Abdo Khal

Winner of the International Prize for Arabic Fiction, this is a hard-hitting and controversial novel set in an opulent palace in Saudi Arabia. Ambitious Tariq dreams of a life there, but dream quickly turns to nightmare.

'Khal writes vividly and poetically … (a) powerful and deeply troubling book' SHOLTO BYRNES, *NATIONAL*

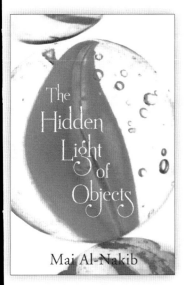

THE HIDDEN LIGHT OF OBJECTS

by Mai al Nakib

If you look beyond the headlines, you might see life in the Middle East as it is really lived – adolescent love, yearnings for independence, the fragility of marriage. Mai Al-Nakib's luminous stories carefully unveil the lives of ordinary people in the Middle East – and the power of ordinary objects to hold extraordinary memories.

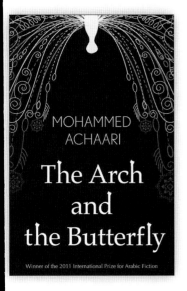

THE ARCH AND THE BUTTERFLY

by Mohammed Achaari

Joint winner of the International Prize for Arabic Fiction, this is a moving novel of identity, extremism, culture and generational change. Youssef, the son of a cross-cultural marriage and a practising leftist shocked by a family tragedy, finds himself questioning everything including his own values and identity.

For more information, please visit www.bqfp.com.qa

ABOVE: People stand on the roof of a destroyed house in Aleppo, Syria

IN FOCUS

In this section

Bordering isolation

43(2): 62/66 | DOI: 10.1177/0306422014536301

Kate Maltby reports on the Doms, nomads who have been forced by the Syrian war into Turkey and "pass" as Kurds to get better treatment

BEFORE THE SYRIAN civil war, 60-year-old Shaima was used to slipping over Turkey's porous eastern border twice a year. "They hated us here, but in the summer there was always work. The men helped with the harvest, and there were weddings for the girls to dance. And at the wedding parties, they'd pay our men for music, then you-know-what with our women. Every winter, we would go back to Aleppo, to the big family." Did she ever have a passport to ease her transit? "Of course not! Haven't the Turks told you, we are gypsies?"

Shaima is a Syrian Dom, a member of a marginal group whose nomadic existence has left her people barely documented and all but invisible in their place of refuge. Today Shaima lives in a refugee camp near Gaziantep, Turkey's sixth-largest city. She is among the 2.5 million people who have fled Syria as civil war ravages the country. As of March 2014, the United Nations High Commissioner for Refugees had documented the arrival of nearly 650,000 Syrian refugees in Turkey. Activist Kemal Vural Tarlan, a photographer who has documented the Dom for the last decade, argues that the true number is nearly double that, and should include hundreds of thousands of unregistered refugees who have illicitly crept or bribed their way across the border and now work in the black economy. The Syrian Dom are among the least likely Syrians to have ID papers,

and all people arriving at the border without papers spend months in spontaneously established border camps, shanty towns in the no-man's land between the spot where Syria ends and Turkey begins, denied entry. Tens of thousands of Syrians are reported to have died of starvation here, just out of reach of refuge.

Since the emergence of jihadist guerilla opposition to the Syrian regime, most importantly ISIS, the Islamic State of Iraq and the Levant, access to much of the border is controlled by Islamist fighters. So the unofficial shanty camps stretching for miles just inside the Turkish border are places of starvation and suspicion. "To bring aid to the starving," claims Vural Tarlan, "you have to be permitted by the jihadis." Shiraz Maher, senior research fellow at King's College London's International Centre for the Study of Radicalisation, has similar tales from the region: "No one can get aid inside the border without the agreement of the IHH." Wildly popular in Turkey, the IHH is an Islamist-leaning organisation that collects funds seemingly for humanitarian aid: it is frequently accused of siphoning its funds to Islamist fighters. In the West, the IHH is mainly known for its role in the 2010 "flotilla raid" to break the Israeli blockade of the Gaza strip. To its defenders, the IHH is merely an Islamic version of Christian Aid; to its detractors, it is a front for terrorism. What is clear is that the

ABOVE: Nomadic Dom musicians in the Amuq plain, close to the Turkish city of Antakya

Syrian Dom are undesirable to Islamists. In regions where access to aid is dependent on perceived piety, the Dom, with their reputation for Alevi theism and promiscuity, rarely make the cut.

Those who do get to eastern Turkey find that ethnic rivalries have preceded them. Broadly speaking, the Turkish population has been welcoming to their Syrian guests: the Turkish government has spent $2 billion on refugee support, and for all the country's political divisions, the cost to the Turkish taxpayer has been accepted with barely a murmur from the opposition. But this gen-

erosity rarely extends to those refugees who swell the numbers of ethnic minorities that Turkey already finds inconvenient. And as the total number of refugees in the country approaches one million, the reluctance in some quarters to integrate Syrians culturally in Turkey is creating a demographic time-bomb.

At present, Turkish officials and Syrian refugee leaders alike choose to murmur about a swift end to the Syrian war and a return home for refugees, ducking questions about how far Syrians should put down roots in Turkey. The ruling AK Party →

proudly boasts that it will pay for any Syrian who meets the entry requirements to attend a Turkish university – but in reality a mere thousand state scholarships have been awarded, because few of the hundreds of thousands young Syrians in the country meet the required proficiency in Turkish.

This is not a hurdle the Turkish government is keen to remove. The question of whether Syrian children should learn Turkish has become a political battle. In a nation which for years denied Kurdish children education in their own tongue, the ministry of education now insists that children in Syrian refugee camps should learn in their own language – and only their own language. In the Gaziantep region's generously funded

At this fault line between two hard-pressed minorities much of the worst violence experienced by the Dom has erupted

network of showpiece refugee camps, the ministry provides schoolbooks based on the Turkish curriculum, but only in Syrian Arabic. Aid agencies talk, off the record, of serious difficulties in encouraging camp governors to provide lessons in Turkish, or even English. Fatima, a Circassian refugee in the flagship Nizip II camp in Gaziantep, told me she had abandoned her post as a volunteer in the camp school in protest against the authorities' refusal to provide even a basic introduction to Turkish for her children. "They told me, why do I need to learn Turkish, when I won't be staying in Turkey? So I said, what is the point of teaching our children at all, if they will never have a life in this country?"

This is not to say Turkish citizenship is off the table for all Syrians: ahead of the April 2014 elections, reports emerged in Gaziantep

of incumbent officials handing out ID cards on condition that the recipients performed their first civic duty by obediently voting AKP.

Meanwhile, as Prime Minister Recep Tayypi Erdogan continues to rally his supporters against those considered insufficiently Islamic, his main targets have been Turkey's Alevi population, a group closely associated with Domari speakers. The Alevi religion combines music and dance: as Hussein, a young Alevi from Istanbul, tells me: "Almost every ritual is a dance – we worship the divine through music and with our bodies."

Alevi religious practices have long fascinated the West, with their Sufi-influenced mysticism lionised as a liberal Islam. Nonetheless, most Alevi traditions quite clearly predate Islam, a fact that is not lost on their Islamist detractors. One of the most significant demonstrations against Erdogan last year, during the Gezi park protests, took place on 2 July, the 20th anniversary of an arson attack on an Alevi conference in which 33 leading intellectuals were killed at Sivas, Istanbul. Two months earlier, Erdogan had announced the name of the latest structure to bridge the Bosphorus: the Yavuz Sultan Selim Bridge, named for Selim the Grim, notorious for massacring Alevis. As Anglo-Turkish author Alev Scott notes in her recent book, Turkish Awakening, Selim famously declared: "The killing of one Alevi has as much heavenly reward as the killing of 70 Christians." On the anniversary of the Sivas massacre, for which no one has been convicted, it felt like a slap in the face.

By no means all of the 10-15 million Alevis in Turkey are Domari speakers, but a majority of Domari speakers are Alevis or, crucially, perceived to be so. In a transitory population, such distinctions between Alevi and Domari, Domari and Kurd, frequently blur. The European Roma Rights Centre (ERRC) claims that Turkey was already home to 500,000 Domari speakers before the Syrian influx, in a combined total of five

million Roma, Dom and Lom "gypsies". But most assimilated Domari speakers go through phases of hiding their ethnic heritage, passing as Kurds when settling in new towns. And it is at this fault line between two hard-pressed minorities that much of the worst violence experienced by the Dom has erupted. In a notorious instance in 2006, two Dom teenagers working as shepherds were lynched in the city of Silvan, shortly before their employers, an impoverished Kurdish farming family, were due to pay them for seven months' work. The local police repeatedly failed to investigate the deaths.

Syria's Dom population is a marginal group whose nomadic existence has left them barely documented and all but invisible in their place of refuge. The question of whether the label "gypsy" should be used for the Dom is one on which ethnologists fiercely disagree – Shaima herself insists that her people have no ethnic relationship to the "criminal" Roma. But here in eastern Turkey, the locals are in no doubt. "Çingene", a regional leader of the ruling AK Party, spits out when asked about provision for the Dom population. And then, reverting to English: "Gypsies. Why do you want to go near them? Anyway, there are none here. They go to dirty places, like Istanbul."

The 2.2 million Dom have always lived on the margins of society. Most Middle East states disclaim the need to provide Domari language support in schools, or seasonal health clinics at Dom campsites. One of the few places to offer them some shelter was Saddam Hussein's Iraq, at some cost to their reputation: a few years ago I met young Iraqis in Istanbul who spoke with nostalgia of Baghdad's red-light Kamalia district, in which Dom women worked as dancers for Saddam's top commanders – and allegedly as courtesans. Since the US invasion in 2003, religious sects have taken turns to purge Baghdad of the Doms' seemingly unIslamic influence: Kamalia has been renamed Hay al-Zahra after the distinctly more virtuous

ABOVE: Two Dom children play as adults collect waste paper, card and scrap iron, in Antep, Turkey

daughter of the Prophet, and in 2005 Reuters and the Dom Research Center reported that the army of Muqtada al-Sadr had unleashed mortar rounds on a makeshift village of 250 Dom families near Diwaniya, killing one and forcing the encampment to disband. "Iraqi leaders of all sects repeat the same line about the Dom people: 'They are alcohol-sellers and whores, so there is no place for them in an Islamic nation,'" says photographer Vural Tarlan. "They can no longer punish Saddam, so they have decided the Dom symbolise his decadence. This is their revenge."

Now it is the turn of Syria's Dom population to be cast adrift. Before the civil war, tens of thousands of Dom made their winter homes in Syria, mainly in Damascus and Aleppo. SIL International, the UNESCO-recognised body which researches endangered languages, claims 37,000 Domari speakers were left in the country in 2005, but linguist Dr Bruno Hérin, one of the world's few experts on the Domari tongue, cautions against exact figures. Vural Tarlan suggests that the number under the radar may be far higher: "There is no official recognition whatsoever, in Syria, just as in Turkey, Lebanon, Jordan or Palestine." So most Syrian Dom have lived in hiding, passing as Kurds for official purposes. Hérin's research suggests that up to 10,000 Domari speakers based themselves in Damascus before the war – alongside scratching a living as musicians, blacksmiths and tinkers, the Dom appear to have cornered the Syrian market in cut-price dentistry. →

→ And that's not all. The ERRC's 2008 report on violence against Roma and Dom populations identified a disturbing pattern of Dom women marrying into Kurdish families, only for their in-laws to respond with violence when they discovered that the new wife was merely "passing". Frequently Dom women are on the receiving end of violence from both their own and neighbouring communities. In a typical instance in 1997, a woman from the town of Van was discovered by her husband's Kurdish family to be of Dom origin – her in-laws expelled her, but her brother escorted her back to her husband's home to avert dishonour. Shortly after, she was found shot to death, almost certainly at the hands of her husband.

In the same town, locals tell the story of a young Dom woman convicted of the murder of her Kurdish husband. At her trial, neighbours testified that a functional marriage had suddenly turned sour when, after seven years, the husband had discovered his wife's Dom origin. He had responded with extreme physical abuse, marking her breasts with scissors and publicly harnessing her to carts.

But for all this doom and gloom, there are growing signs of Dom-Kurd integration throughout eastern Turkey. A century after the genocide, the old Armenian quarter in Gaziantep once again bustles with life. The Armenian quarter is long gone, but its narrow houses are home to an assortment of Kurds, Dom and Syrian refugees, living alongside each other. Together, they form the city's second economy: Gaziantep, one of the world's fastest growing cities, is hungry for cheap labour to support its booming agricultural industry. So when Turks come home to sleep, the refugees go out to cover the nightshift in farms and factories.

In a quiet alley in this quarter is Kemal Vural Tarlan's Kirkayak Arts Centre. It is the only place in Gaziantep you can watch an independent film – and the locus of a project to forge a new relationship between Kurds and the Dom travellers they have so long resented. Vural Tarlan is a Kurd. He tries to give Dom refugees a voice through phototherapy: every weekend he holds workshops for the Dom community, teaching them to use a camera, and encouraging them to take photographs of their experiences throughout the week. "These people are travellers," he says. "They come to my workshops for two months, three months, then they move out of town. But when I print their photographs, I find they have left something permanent behind." He regularly holds exhibitions dedicated to Dom photography in universities throughout Turkey, visual campaigns to remind Turks of the forgotten communities living alongside them.

But Vural Tarlan doesn't just give the Dom people artistic representation. His arts centre is a hub for the Kurdish community in Gaziantep – and it is through him that Gaziantep's Kurds find themselves meeting the despised Dom people as equals, neighbours, even artistic partners. Vural Tarlan believes things are improving between the two groups, citing regional government efforts in neighbouring Diyarbakır to ensure hate crimes reported by the Dom are followed up by police. In a region under intense demographic pressure, racial tensions are not going away any time soon. But leaving Vural Tarlan's workshop, surrounded by self-portraits of smiling, confident Dom children, it is hard not to feel hopeful. ☒

Some names in this article have been changed

©Kate Maltby
www.indexoncensorship.org

Kate Maltby has travelled widely in Turkey as a classical scholar. She writes on politics for the Daily Telegraph in the UK, and is completing a PhD at University College London. She tweets @katemaltby

Pakistan at a crossroads

43(2): 67/70 | DOI: 10.1177/0306422014535533

Amid rising extremism and intense local powerplay, how do ordinary Pakistani voters make decisions? Political scientist and author **Haroon K Ullah** spent eight years carrying out on-the-ground research for his latest book. Here he writes about the tensions that dominate daily life

ISLAMABAD TREMBLED, AND I felt the reverberating fear first-hand. It was 4 January 2011, and another high-profile politician had been killed. I was living a few blocks from Kohsar Market, the upscale international bazaar that catered mostly to foreign visitors, expatriates and corporate types. The neighbourhood is considered one of the safest in the capital. That afternoon, Salmaan Taseer, governor of Punjab, the nation's most populous province, and a well-known political player, ate lunch with a friend at the market. Throughout his career, Taseer was outspoken in his belief that democracy and pluralism were inseparable, advocating that all religious minorities (including non-Muslims) should be allowed equal voting rights in the country's general elections. But such progressive ideas were anathema to the Islamists. Shortly before his death, Taseer had outraged the Islamists by criticising Pakistan's strict blasphemy laws, calling them unjust and indefensible. He had spoken out in defence of a Christian woman, Aasiya Bibi, who was convicted under the blasphemy laws and given a long prison sentence. Taseer argued that the extremists were abusing the blasphemy laws and that Islamic law should not supplant state laws.

As a consequence, over the years, Taseer received numerous death threats. He showed true moral courage by refusing to be silenced. After lunch that day he was murdered by a member of his own security detail. He died where he fell.

The rise of extremist political groups in Pakistan is of great international significance. Poised, with a fully loaded nuclear arsenal, at the crossroads of religious fundamentalism, nationalist fervour, and the war on terror, Pakistan's importance to global geopolitical stability and international peace is inescapable. While Pakistan's political landscape still depends on military patronage, its current democratic transition will depend on how political parties contribute to civilian rule and mobilise support for political reform. Voters are stuck between a series of tough choices. The most under-studied aspects of key political stakeholders in Pakistan are political parties, especially those that use religion to leverage their agenda. How do common voters make decisions about who to follow? What is the role of religion in these decisions?   →

ABOVE: The face of Mumtaz Qadri, the bodyguard who murdered Salmaan Taseer for speaking out against Pakistan's blasphemy laws, is carried on a banner. Members of various political parties demonstrated against Qadri's sentence for Taseer's murder in Karachi, 2011

Credit: Akhtar Soomro/Reuters

→ The majority of Pakistanis come into contact with the state – and, by extension, formal politics – via the mediation of their landlord. Many rural workers owe their livelihoods to wealthy land barons, who control their votes. Landlords may or may not be politicians themselves, but they do participate in politics on the provincial or national level, usually by promising

The combination of landlord power and religious politics is a powerful dynamic

the votes of their local faction to a politician who, in turn, provides the village with services.

On the village level, therefore, landlords fulfill many of the roles that are normally associated with the state, including securing and spending public development funds and assisting villagers in navigating bureaucracy. Landlords' connections to provincial-level politicians, who are connected to national-

level power brokers, allow them to obtain and distribute such important favours as jobs. The combination of landlord power and religious politics is a powerful dynamic.

Political scientist Stathis Kalyvas has defined "confessional" political parties as organisations that leverage aspects of religious ideology and culture to mobilise, recruit and campaign in electoral contests. Pakistan is not alone in having confessional parties. Confessional movements have developed out of many religious traditions in many countries. Jews in Israel, Christians in Brazil, and Hindus in India have all formed political parties whose platforms draw from and focus on religious tradition. Islamic confessional movements, however, are of particular interest in the post-9/11 world. Pakistan has several new trends, especially with regards to the information explosion, voter sophistication and party organisational behaviour.

With over 80 TV channels and over 100 million with access to TV, the explosion in information has fundamentally changed politics in Pakistan. Information on

ABOVE: A woman knits a mat outside her home in Saidpur village, Islamabad. Village landlords act as political intermediaries and fulfil many of the roles normally associated with the state

political activities and mobilisation is now ubiquitous. Parties can cater towards niche voters that are watching their specific TV channel. In fact, Islamic political organisations frequently engage in political strategies that require them to condone actions, including violence, and form coalitions with militant and secular organisations that run contrary to their own platforms. Recognising that these organisations are as tethered to practical political considerations has huge implications for our understanding of what drives political extremism and how to create incentives for moderation.

While debate over the proper role of Islam still rages in Pakistan, people there generally accept the overlap between affairs of state and of the soul. The separation between religion and politics, considered so desirable in Western democracies, simply does not exist in Pakistan. The "hand of Allah" and references to God's will are seen and felt everywhere. The Pakistani constitution begins, "In the name of God, the Beneficent and the Merciful." Confessional parties use slogans like "Islam is the solution". Banners on election booths remind voters, "Islam is our destiny, in this life and the hereafter." The Pakistani legal system incorporates aspects of sharia with its sharia courts, religious laws governing marriage and inheritance, and the infamous blasphemy laws, which ban defamatory speech against Islam or its prophet Mohammed. Children in public schools all over Pakistan are required to memorise Bilad-e-Islamia, a poem by Muhammad Iqbal that deplores political leaders who tout themselves as Muslims but are devoid of a genuine spiritual attachment to the prophet.

Research shows Islamist parties that are successful on the local level stand to gain material, social and organisational benefits. For one, control over the local levels of government, including the offices of *nazim* (mayor) and *patwari* (local record keeper) confers a huge amount of authority over land distribution and ownership, still the central component of class standing in Paki-

stan's pseudo-feudal economy. Local political power also drives membership and fundraising for the local religious institutions that sponsor and staff Islamist political parties. Religious authority and political authority are mutually reinforcing in rural districts, so it makes sense for organisations that have religious origins to engage in electoral competition at that level. For rural political entrepreneurs, national elections may be of little relevance, at least compared to the direct benefits of winning local control.

The work of Dr Matthew Nelson, of the Centre for the Study of Pakistan at London's School of Oriental and African Studies, on politician-constituent relations in Punjab province provides specific examples of how the patron-client relationships function in Pakistani politics. Nelson shows that most rural Punjabis assess their representatives, whether on the local or national level, not on the politicians' ability to craft and promote new legislation that will advance the people's interests but on their ability to help them avoid the impact of Pakistan's laws on the inheritance of land. Since the 1970s and Zia's Islamisation campaign, these laws have been gradually changed to better reflect Islam's insistence that female heirs receive a share of the land, but the changes have brought them into direct conflict with tribal custom, which dictates only males inherit land. Nelson's survey of local landowners and district court cases found that constituents believe the politicians' most important job is to craft out-of-court settlements and →

→ keep lawsuits out of the courts. As far as land law is concerned, the most important politician in a village may not be the district's member of the National Assembly but the *patwari*, who, for a fee, can alter the records of land ownership in a particular citizen's favour. By arranging for their clients to avoid the mandates of Pakistani law (whether in questions of land distribution or merely passing through customs at the airport), politicians show that they are "stronger than rules". Their influence attracts more clients, who in turn increase their political power.

By contrast, in urban areas the *nazim* does not distribute land, nor is land ownership of such huge significance. Local religious institutions are not the sole authority here,

For rural entrepreneurs, national elections are of little relevance, compared to the benefits of winning local control

nor are religious leaders even close to the most powerful elites. For the Muslim democratic political entrepreneur in an urban centre, local elections simply are not worth the investment. For these actors and organisations, the better payoff is at the national-level elections. Muslim democratic parties are the product of ancient aristocracies and efforts by a relatively small number of feudal lords and their families to protect their feudal rule over land, wealth and power. With the rise of suffrage, that system has morphed into a form of patronage democracy in which the National Assembly has control over the dispersal of desirable material goods, services and jobs. Traditional elites maintain their political, economic and social power through their access to the state and consequent ability to distribute or withhold patronage. Electoral success at the national level also gives Muslim democrats a platform to espouse policies that may appeal to targeted voters, but parlia-

mentary inefficacy protects them from having to address the actual implementation or the practical consequences of those policies.

Pakistan's current political climate is marked by uncertainty and upheaval. The Taliban's move into the northwest tribal regions and more settled areas of Pakistan has changed the geopolitical landscape; traditional political alliances and affiliations are facing real challenges. Muslim democrats are threatened by the neo-Taliban expansion. While the Punjabi Taliban are interested in a different set of issues, their geographic proximity with democrats means they are now competing for supporters. Interestingly, as a result of the neo-Taliban expansion, even some Islamist parties now share interests with the state. In Sindh, the Jamaat-e-Islami fears the Taliban incursion because it will reduce its support among the Urdu-speaking Mujahir urban population. The Jamiat Ulema-e-Islam (JUI), meanwhile, is reluctant to say anything publicly about the Taliban. The party highly values the perception of being a mediator. If the JUI was seen as leaning too heavily in the other direction, they would fear Taliban excursions into their own power bases in the northern areas.

The Taliban have been able to carve out a political role given the geographic electoral politics and international issues in Afghanistan. In short, the rise of the Taliban and violent terrorist groups is resulting in major changes in Pakistan's historical political alliances. Landowners and religious entrepreneurs have never been more powerful. ☒

© Haroon K. Ullah
www.indexoncensorship.org

Haroon K. Ullah is a scholar, diplomat and field researcher specialising in south Asia and the Middle East. He serves on US Secretary of State John Kerry's policy planning staff, focusing on public diplomacy and countering violent extremism. His latest novel is The Bargain from the Bazaar (Public Affairs)

Spying on the censors

43(2): 71/74 | DOI: 10.1177/0306422014536111

Metadata helps spies to keep tabs on their targets but it can be used to reveal censorship too, as **Roger Highfield** reports

SIMPLY PUT, METADATA is data about data and, in the wake of recent revelations about the US National Security Agency collecting oceans of the stuff, there has been understandable alarm about what such data can reveal about you without the need to listen in to your phone calls or rummage through your emails.

But, in the light of a new analysis, metadata might also offer fascinating opportunities to spy on the censors who spy on us.

Metadata is pervasive. It is written into a digital photo file, for example, to identify who owns it, how large the image is, copyright information and keywords about it. Web pages and video files also carry metadata to describe their content, although most people don't see it. Text files are imprinted with information about when they were created, their author, plus a summary. And so on.

By far the most common uses of all this metadata are relatively benign, though they can be annoying. Many companies use metadata to reveal our habits, interests and connections to work out what we buy, where we go online and who we talk to, so we can be targeted with hints, suggestions and advertising.

When you send or receive text messages by mobile or Twitter or third-party apps, a huge amount can be deduced. Add in a phone's location data and email metadata

and it is easy to see whom you work with (activity in office hours), who you like to hang out with or are related to (lots of calls) and where you like to relax (activity in the evenings).

Facebook can reveal a lot too. The Mirror project, devised by the National Media Museum in Bradford, creative agency RKCR/Y&R and Cambridge University Psychometrics Centre, can deduce much about a person's personality. The tool, which relied on extensive research by the Cambridge team comprising more than six million test results and in excess of four million individual profiles, could use "likes" to make a pretty good guess about a user's traits, gender and age.

Every tweet comes loaded with metadata, and if they're geotagged or have images, that data should show up, too. However, there may also be opportunities to use this data to scan for state monitoring and censorship of microblogs, such as Twitter and China's Sina Weibo, according to work carried out by Donn Morrison at the Digital Enterprise Research Institute (now known as Insight) in Galway, Ireland.

Through various networks we can now interact with players all over the world, from friends and family to business partners and colleagues, courtesy of the telephone, email, or the internet. Though these networks look haphazard, they do contain mathematical structure.

ABOVE: Spying in the 21st century rarely involves guns and high-speed car chases. A more realistic James Bond (portrayed here by Daniel Craig) would spend far more time staring at computers

→ Scientific study of this "small world" idea dates back to investigations by US social psychologist Stanley Milgram at Harvard University in the 1960s. In one experiment, he sent a package to 160 people randomly

It could be possible to create an app that uses metadata to send an alert when the authorities are tampering with posts

selected in Omaha, Nebraska, asking them to forward it to a friend or acquaintance whom they thought would help bring the package closer to a target person, a stock-broker who lived in Boston, Massachusetts. Amazingly, given the many millions of people living in the US, his experiment suggested there tended to be six people on average linking any one person with another – giving rise to the popular notion that we all may be connected by just six degrees of separation.

Then came an interesting study putting Milgram's observations into a theoretical framework. Duncan Watts of Columbia University and Steven Strogatz of Cornell University came up with a mathematical model to show that the six degrees of separation idea works because in every small group of friends, websites, power grids or whatever there are a few people, sites, hubs and other nodes that have much wider connections, either across continents or across social divisions. Albert-László Barabási at Northeastern University, Boston, then took the idea further, highlighting that the distribution of network's links approximates to what scientists call a "power law", or a so-called exponential distribution. This sees a tiny fraction of nodes receiving a hugely disproportionate share of links, while the vast majority is mostly ignored. These networks have a small number of hubs that are significantly more connected than the other nodes in the network. The bottom line of all this research is that online social networks do have deep mathematical regularities.

When Morrison, who is now at the Norwegian University of Science and Technology, simulated on a virtual network the actions of state censors who deleted some 10 per cent of posts, he found the missing links altered the shape of the entire network, leaving it malformed and less connected. This was especially true with popular posts that had been retweeted, which of course are the ones that are more likely to be spotted by the censors.

From the shifts in the network topology (ie the arrangement of its nodes and connecting lines), Morrison was able to spot when censorship was taking place on a →

What is metadata?

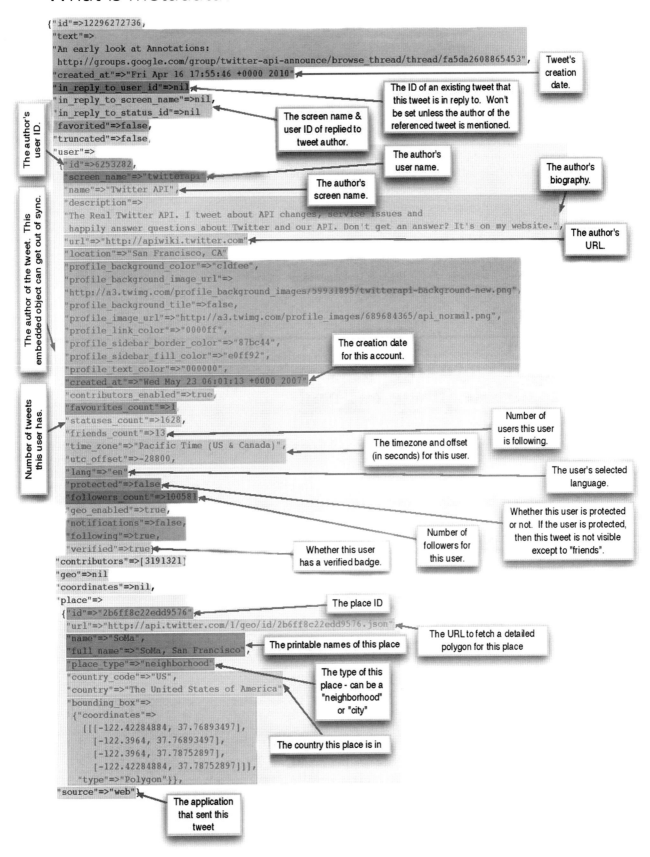

ABOVE: This diagram, created by Raffi Krikorian at Twitter, shows what is revealed from the metadata of one Tweet

→ wide scale, with 85 per cent accuracy. That means it could be possible to create an app that uses metadata to send an alert when the authorities are tampering with posts.

China is one country where this kind of censorship takes place. Research published in 2012 revealed that 16 per cent of all Sina Weibo posts had been deleted and that censorship of messages originating in areas of potential unrest, such as Tibet, occurred in more than half of cases.

Morrison's work complements related projects. ConceptDoppler, under development by a team at the University of California, Davis, can spot information that is filtered for keywords as it passes along routers through browser toolbars, email, Twitter or Herdict.org.

When crowdsourced information about internet filtering, denial of service attacks, and other blockages is blended with a judicious pinch of metadata, then the larger scale uses of censorship, for reasons of politics, morality or whatever, will be more transparent than ever before. X

© Roger Highfield
www.indexoncensorship.org

Sensitive word lists play an important role in the cat-and-mouse game of censorship and circumvention

on the internet, for instance by the "Great Firewall of China", which blocks a range of websites.

Morrison says that sensitive word lists play an important role in the cat-and-mouse game of censorship and circumvention, but the network structure also offers some interesting new opportunities to detect and quantify censorship. Indeed, weighing up the impact of censorship on Twitter, LinkedIn and Facebook this way could turn out to be much easier to do than tracking lists of sensitive words, such as "dictator", "anarchy" and "riot", which may change depending on what is going through the mind of online censors at any one time.

Studies of metadata could also complement the more traditional reports sent to the Herdict project at Harvard University. When individuals can't access a site, or have evidence of deleted Tweets and posts, they can report that experience to Herdict

Roger Highfield is director of external affairs at the Science Museum Group. He is former science editor of The Daily Telegraph and former editor of the New Scientist

Going in deep

43(2): 75/79 | DOI: 10.1177/0306422014536488

Tackling the big issues as a journalist in Tanzania can involve putting your life on the line, as recent attacks have shown. **Erick Kabendera** and **Jess McCabe** look at a project helping provide the funds and confidence for investigative reporting

WHEN JOURNALIST RAMADHANI Mbwaduke came across a story of corruption within the Tanzanian government, it was no simple question of "publish and be damned".

Tanzania can be a scary place for a journalist. Physical attacks on members of the press have escalated over the last few years, and combined with government shutdowns of publications that run critical stories, and lack of resources, getting an investigative story published is no mean feat. Freedom House considers that Tanzania has a "partly free" press. But, as the experiences of Tanzanian journalists reveal, the difference between "partly free" and "entirely free" can be large.

"The attacks on journalists make me feel scared to write controversial stories. I know some stories could easily get you killed," says Mbwaduke. "And you can't be a brave journalist if you are dead."

While conducting desktop research one morning in March last year, Mbwaduke discovered discrepancies in how two districts in southern Tanzania – Kilwa and Mtwara rural districts – were spending levies paid to them by a firm extracting natural gas.

"The Kilwa district council's financial reports indicated that a large part of the money had been used to build the council director's house, given to a women's credit cooperative and to repair a gravel driveway at an exorbitant price, while nothing was allocated to repair a health centre's broken building and buy medicine for patients. I felt it was important to find out whether the money had reached the projects mentioned in the financial reports," says Mbwaduke.

Mbwaduke works as a reporter at Nipashe, one of the biggest national Swahili daily newspapers. Although his editors wanted key stories investigated and published, funds remained a constraint. A research trip to the countryside can cost £300, and low circulation figures meant very little cash for investigative stories. A quality daily newspaper in Tanzania might have a circulation of about 25,000, compared to about 250,000 in Kenya (even though both countries have similar-sized populations).

This is where the Tanzania Media Fund (TMF) comes into play. TMF was founded in 2008, with money from the Swiss and British governments. Kenny Ferguson, a spokesperson for the Department for International Development (Dfid), explains: "It is a programme that seeks to support quality journalism that better informs the public, contributes to debate and increases public demand for greater accountability across Tanzania. It focuses on investigative journalism and public interest journalism." Dfid →

ABOVE: Controversial stories don't often make it into Tanzania's newspapers

→ has invested £842m in the fund, with a commitment to invest an additional £2m by 2016, one of a handful of the little-publicised UK government projects funding journalism in other countries.

Dfid did not respond to requests for substantive comment about the impetus behind such schemes. But the Swiss government, another TMF donor, was more forthcoming.

Apart from individual grants provided to journalists, TMF also offers institutional transformation grants. Online media platform Jamii Forums/Fikra Pevu attracts close to one million visitors daily, more than all daily newspapers combined. Recently they received funds to hire professional journalists and move operations from a garage to an office.

"The chance for the media to contribute to positive change depends on objective and quality reporting," says Geraldine Zeuner, a director for development cooperation from the Swiss Development Corporation.

In fact, most of the stories funded by TMF appear to steer cautiously clear of hot topics, such as government corruption.

Christoph Spurk, a Swiss consultant, carried out a qualitative analysis of stories written by the journalists supported by TMF, and found that only 8 per cent of stories uncovered wrongdoing by public officials. For context, Dfid has committed to donating £633m to Tanzania between 2011 and 2016, much in direct bilateral aid to the government.

Yet the outcome for journalists working in a financially precarious and potentially dangerous climate has been the opportunity to write robust stories, rather than propaganda.

Mbwaduke, knowing that his newspaper was unable to facilitate his investigation, decided to take the idea to the TMF who offered to him £560 to cover his expenses to travel to the countryside and write the story. TMF also assigned him one of 15 mentors – experienced Tanzanian journalists – to guide him throughout the process.

Mbwaduke says he was able to investigate the story for three months. "The guidance I received from the mentor was priceless; he helped me stay focused on the main issues of the story. Because the mentor is a very experienced journalist, his previous work also motivated me to follow in his footsteps," he says.

As a result, he was able to break out of the practice of conducting interviews by phone from the country's biggest city, Dar es Salaam, where almost all major national newspapers are based.

Most of the 11-part series that resulted from his investigation, exposing how the council's administration abused the funds, appeared on the front page of Nipashe newspaper. Mbwaduke says the impact was felt immediately after the stories came out.

Publishing such a story was a risk. But, in this case, it paid off. First, Mdwaduke received a surprise call from the council's director who was the main culprit of the

The chance for the media to contribute to positive change depends on objective and quality reporting

scandal, thanking him for exposing the wrongdoing.

Shortly afterwards, ordinary people who had read the stories called to inform him that a health centre had now been refurbished and medicine was being provided to the patients. The country's corruption watchdog had also started investigating the matter. The director, together with other senior officials implicated in the scandal, was moved to another area.

"I didn't know how to use multiple sources of information while investigating a story. I would ordinarily speak to two people and write a story. But I interviewed 50 people for the story and the interviews helped me understand the subject I was writing about. I also felt professional →

|||||||||||||||||||||||||||||||||||||||||||||||||

In numbers

....

UK government funding of journalists world-
wide. Source: DFID tracker
Democratic Republic of the Congo: £12.8m
Iraq: £10.1m
Tanzania: £2.8m
Angola: £995,000

→ satisfaction for exposing how civil servants were abusing public funds and action
was taken against them," he says.

Because of the impact the story had,
Mbwaduke says his newspaper decided to
replicate TMF's technique whereby each
reporter is encouraged to submit a unique
news idea to editors. Each journalist whose
idea gets approved is assigned to an editor
to guide him or her through the process of
researching and writing the story. The newspaper also gives money to reporters to travel
to different parts of the country to investigate their story ideas.

The scale of this change may seem small
– giving journalists expenses so they can
travel and report on their stories. Additional
resources being ploughed into newsrooms
does not in itself provide extra protections
against censorship or the suppression of
journalists. But it is a small and practical
step towards reporting important stories that
uncover corruption, inform the public and
incite change. ⊠

© Erick Kabendera and Jess McCabe
www.indexoncensorship.org

Erick Kabendera is a journalist based in Dar
es Salaam, Tanzania
Jess McCabe is a British journalist and editor
of the F Word

Life as a journalist in Tanzania

Erick Kabendera tells Index about violent attacks on colleagues, and how his writing led to his elderly parents being arrested and three break-ins to his home

When a former colleague called me at 5am in early March last year, I sensed something was wrong.

He broke the sad news that a friend, mentor and senior journalist Absalom Kibanda, was in hospital fighting for his life after unidentified people attacked him outside of his house.

Luckily, he was flown to South Africa for advanced medical attention and survived, but many other journalists don't.

A few weeks before the attack, my elderly parents had been arrested by authorities and asked to tell me to "be careful with stories". My house was broken into three times and I was questioned about my citizenship.

Around that time, a TV journalist, Daudi Mwangosi, who was covering a banned opposition party rally, was shot dead by riot police. Shortly afterwards a radio journalist, covering a controversial story, was found hanged in the bush. Many more were harassed and threatened.

In the last three years, three influential Swahili-language national newspapers have been banned. Two of them, which were shut down for reporting about new salaries for civil servants, have since been allowed to publish again, but another one, which revealed the identify of an undercover agent who allegedly killed the leader of a doctors' strike, remains out of business.

Things haven't improved but there is a crop of young journalists who are committed to the profession, but lack role models and are poorly paid.

A writer I am mentoring at the Tanzania Media Fund (TMF) was about to quit journalism before he joined a three-month programme that gives young journalists the opportunities to investigate stories of their choice.

He worked for a small radio station in the north of the country and felt his career wasn't growing. He wanted to do something else, but I persuaded him to carry on, telling him the profession needed young people like him.

A story he had previously worked on won a national award, and a national radio station noticed his talent and employed him. His recent story – about the killing of elderly people suspected of being witches – broke new ground.

When I am mentoring young journalists, I see a lot of energy and determination, yet also fear to do stories that would not make the government happy. Most of them lack role models to encourage them to become independent in their thinking. Sometimes government officials deny them information for stories if they feel the stories don't suit their political interests.

Those who are brave, lack exposure and the essential skills to communicate effectively. Newsrooms rarely invest in training and career development of reporters.

Over the years, most good journalists have left the profession to work in public relations. Media outlets have resorted to using poorly educated journalists who are underpaid. Most of these indulge in extortion activities from news sources to make a living.

TMF has done good work to show it is possible to have a vibrant and independent media. But media outlets have to take the initiative into their hands to make such efforts sustainable even when the fund is gone. Media owners need to invest more in their outlets and efforts to force the government to protect newspapers and their journalists.

© Erick Kabendera
www.indexoncensorship.org

Erick Kabendera is a journalist, based in Dar es Salaam, Tanzania

Open books

43(2): 80/83 | DOI: 10.1177/0306422014534593

Critics and cynics have long been expecting to relegate libraries to history. But despite funding cuts and technological challenges, many – particularly in Germany – are thriving, forward-looking public spaces, vital for the exchange of ideas, says **Susanne Metz**

ADRAWING FROM THE 1990s by the German cartoonist Til Mette shows a gap between two buildings. A boy sits in front of the empty space, as an elderly man passes by. The man asks with surprise: "Isn't this the place where the public library used to be?" The boy answers: "It is all saved to diskette now."

Fast-forward 20 years and it's the diskettes, not the public libraries, that have become the thing of the past. According to the latest report by the Pew Research Center's Internet and American Life Project, 54 per cent of Americans aged 16 and above had visited a library or mobile library in the past 12 months. In the same year, 288 million library visits were recorded in the UK and about 210 million in Germany. By comparison, 17 million football fans attended a match of the Bundesliga, the German football league, which is the most visited league in the world.

In Germany, modern libraries are the new town halls. They are central, neutral and atmospherically inviting – places where people of all generations and ethnicities can mix. In Berlin and Leipzig, events programmes have included debates on urban development and a range of other political issues, from a proposed cycle network to the impacts of

asylum policy. Libraries in Berlin's Kreuzberg district have played a significant role in encouraging intercultural exchange, by hosting a Tibetan new year's celebration, multicultural family days and breakfast meetings for women from the Turkish community. Leipzig public library has also offered a platform to writers persecuted in their home countries.

But could these activities take place just as well in other places, as German national newspapers have suggested in recent months? "Libraries have no right to exist any longer" was the bold headline in an article by Kathrin Passig on Zeit.de at the end of 2013. Passig called libraries "paper museums" that nobody needs in the age of the internet. The article caused a stir, not only among experts, and was fiercely condemned. Strangely, the author inadvertently appeared to reveal that she had not visited a library for years – if she had she would have experienced a place crowded with young people reading, learning, surfing the internet and talking to each other. On the other hand, some criticism is valid: a large number of libraries do still remain outdated and poorly equipped. Sometimes they lack innovative staff. Above all, they lack the money for innovation, as policymakers do

ABOVE: Seattle Central Library was designed as a "living room" for the city

not recognise what modern, citizen-centric libraries can offer.

In the UK, the reputation of libraries has suffered and funding has been slashed. According to 2012-13 figures published by the Chartered Institute of Public Finance and Accountancy, more than 70 UK libraries closed in that period, making a total of some 200 closures since 2010. Book stock fell too, and there was a year-on-year decline of 6 per cent in visits. The drop is often presented as evidence that libraries are falling out of fashion, but a dip in numbers is inevitable with a reduction in the number of libraries.

In recent years, the socio-spatial appeal of libraries has been highlighted by widely acclaimed new buildings. Seattle Central Library, an incredibly bold, geometric glass building, opened in 2004. Architects Rem Koolhaas and Joshua Ramus reinvented the public library as a "living room" for the city, featuring hundreds of computers and plenty of space for reading. Other spectacular examples of new libraries can, or will, be seen in Singapore, Amsterdam, Stockholm, Stuttgart, Almere and Birmingham. Coming in late 2014, Aarhus library in Denmark, which bills itself as the "Library of Tomorrow", will have →

ABOVE: Relaxing in the children's library in Leipzig

→ a prime waterfront location, a state-of-the-art car park, a children's library and creative labs. All of these premises stand

In an ever-changing technological and social environment, libraries are having to adapt to survive and maintain their role in people's lives

out for their architecture and innovative services – from fully automated lending systems and seven-day-a-week opening through

to language and computer courses and "maker spaces" (meeting places for techies). Berlin also has plans to include a new central library, costing around €300m, as part of the redevelopment of a former airfield in the heart of the city.

But in an ever-changing technological and social environment, libraries are having to adapt to survive and maintain their role in people's lives. They are being forced to negotiate an increasing number of obstacles – technological, financial and legal. Many metropolitan libraries around the world have already made changes, for instance, by offering downloadable e-books on their websites via online catalogues or through specific apps. The e-books typically expire automatically at the end of the loan period and do not have to be returned. Thus the library has become a 24/7 service, with the potential to reach many more users – especially when also using social media to promote their services and events.

What now seems to happen at the click of the button hasn't been easy to put into place. Libraries are still trying to negotiate a potential minefield of rights issues. Some publishers will not sell e-books to public libraries; others impose serious restrictions. The same e-book can have different publishers in different countries, so you may see an e-book on an American or British library's website but the same title won't be available to Canadian or German libraries. Ensuring compatibility with a wide range of different e-readers is also a major challenge.

Traditionally, libraries have had control over their own collections, deciding what books to buy and offer for public lending. But now some publishers say rights holders should decide how and where to extend access to a specific work. "Should this interpretation prevail, this would mean that publishers, and not librarians, primarily decide on digital collections in libraries," says the European Bureau of Library Information and Documentation Associations (EBLIDA). "This would mean that libraries would no longer be able to guarantee free access to content, information, and culture." The EBLIDA's current campaign, The Right to e-Read, calls on policymakers to harmonise legal frameworks, particularly on copyright, across Europe. There is concern that if libraries do not provide free access to e-books, people who cannot afford them will be excluded and the digital divide will become even wider.

With digital services of such enormous importance, some argue that there is no need for libraries to have physical locations. But libraries are esteemed as a non-commercial "third place" – neither "home" nor "work" – which offer comfortable environments for reading, meeting, working and relaxing. Libraries, at their best, provide one of the few centres for communities that are politically neutral, non-commercial and open to everyone. Libraries foster participation and help to strengthen democracy. For those reasons alone they should be protected from public sector budget cuts.

In the words of the writer Neil Gaiman: "Libraries really are the gates to the future. We have an obligation to support libraries. To use libraries, to encourage others to use libraries, to protest the closure of libraries. If you do not value libraries, then you do not value information or culture or wisdom. You are silencing the voices of the past and you are damaging the future." ☒

© Susanne Metz
www.indexoncensorship.org

Susanne Metz is the director of Leipzig public libraries in Germany

Legal divisions

43(2): 84/87 | DOI: 10.1177/0306422014537174

While libel tourists have flocked to London, in France levels of libel damages are very low, says lawyer **Dominique Mondoloni**. He looks at the differences in defamation laws on each side of the Channel

ROBERT FAURISSON IS a notorious Holocaust denier. He has been convicted for it several times in French courts. France, like many countries in continental Europe, has adopted laws that criminalise Holocaust denial.

Under French law that doesn't mean people should be allowed to libel him. A recent publication called Faurisson a "falsifier" and a "counterfeiter of history" – statements that in English law would be considered defamatory, though they would be defensible in court. Yet on 16 January, the Paris district court simply dismissed his action for libel. Why? Because in his lawsuit, Faurisson did not argue that these statements were defamatory but that they were insulting.

Unlike English law, French law distinguishes two different types of libel: defamation proper, the imputation or allegation of a fact that damages the reputation of a person or an institution; and insults, which do not contain the imputation or allegation of a fact. Claimants must choose the legal ground on which they act. If he or she mischaracterises a claim, it will be dismissed. The reason for this? The possibility of proving truth. A defamatory statement can be proven true; an insulting statement cannot be proven because it doesn't contain the imputation or allegation of a fact. Saying someone is "a dirty pig" is an insult. It can't be proven true.

Saying someone "harasses employees in the work place" is defamation. It can be proven.

The UK's 2013 Defamation Act includes a new defence of truth, which requires the defendant to prove the "essential truth of the sting of the libel". French courts, however, will accept a defamation defence based on a claim of truth only if the proof submitted by the defendant is considered full, complete and entirely correlated to all the material elements of a defamatory statement. The evidence must, moreover, be contemporaneous to publication. The test of truth is, therefore, more rigorous in France than in England.

But, although in France truth, like the English common law defence of justification (replaced with the defence of truth in the 2013 Defamation Act), is a general defence to an action for defamation, it is not admissible as a defence if the facts concern a person's privacy.

And this is probably one of the most distinguishing features of French law compared with English. France has laws that protect privacy that go beyond the provisions of Article 8 of the European Convention on Human Rights. If London has been called "the libel capital of the world" because of its "notoriously claimant-friendly environment in which to sue" – the words of the lawyer Mark Stephens – it could be said that Paris is the privacy capital of the world. French

ABOVE: French privacy laws protect individuals' rights to their own image, so photos are often blurred to mask the faces of bystanders

privacy law is notably protective of the rights of individuals, including their rights to their own image, which prevents the publication of unauthorised photographs. This is why, for example, newspapers blur the faces of bystanders in photographs.

Other notable differences between the French and English defamation laws are the result of the differences in legal cultures and practices. In his 1872 Notes on England, the French critic Hippolyte Taine describes a typical English trial in which the barristers examine and cross-examine witnesses: "The whole burden of the case falls upon the barristers and the judge is there to check and control them, prohibit certain questions, and act as moderator to the two champions." By contrast, he says, French lawyers

It could be said that Paris is the privacy capital of the world

are "mere phrase-spinners". His description remains, 142 years later, strikingly accurate. The French and English legal systems are radically different, and the format of trials reflects this. France has a legal system based on written law, and the law of libel is →

→ entirely contained in a single statute: the law of 29 July 1881 "on the freedom of the press". Defamation cases are heard by a judge, not by a jury. There is no right to a trial by jury, and the judge does not have the discretion to order one.

Contesting a libel case in the French courts is typically much less expensive than in England – and the damages awarded by French courts for libel are generally low. It is rare that a claimant gets more than €10,000, and symbolic awards for €1 are commonplace.

Partly because of the relatively low level of damages awarded, France has never been confronted with the controversies that led to the recent amendments to English defama-

Contesting a libel case in French courts is typically less expensive than in England – and the damages awarded by French courts are generally low

tion law. In the 2013 Defamation Act, the UK Parliament imposed a "serious harm" test: individuals have to show serious harm to their reputation, companies have to show serious financial harm. The rationale behind this is that it is necessary to deter rich corporate bodies and individuals from using the threat of an expensive libel case over a minor detail as a means of gagging the media. In France, the threat of a libel action is simply not an issue. It has no chilling effect. This is one reason why investigative reporting has thrived in France. Political scandals are routinely reported, even when their newsworthiness is debatable.

Although French libel law is, in practice, more lenient than in England, it is predominantly a matter of criminal law and defamation is a criminal offence. (The offence of criminal libel was effectively abolished in

the UK in 2009 after years of disuse.) Publishing a libel is punished, when the plaintiff is a private person, by a maximum fine of €12,000. But in some cases, libel can be punished by imprisonment, up to one year, and a maximum fine of €45,000 – notably when the defamatory statement concerns the racial origin, colour or sexual orientation of a person or group of persons.

Like England, France allows defences based on truth (*excuse de vérité*) and privilege (*immunité*). Qualified privilege defences are, however, considered in French law as an element in a broader "good faith defence". There is a presumption in French law that all defamatory statements are made with the intention to cause harm to the claimant and that all defamatory statements are made in "bad faith". The defendant is, however, entitled to prove that he or she did not act in bad faith. The success of the defence rests on four cumulative criteria: the objectivity of the presentation; the prudence in the expression (both of which include, for journalists, a careful verification of the sources); the absence of personal animosity towards the plaintiff; and the legitimacy of the goal pursued by the defendant (which includes public interest and artistic, literary, scientific or historical critique). The *droit de critique* in literary, artistic and scientific matters is a subset of the general "good faith" defence. Something very similar has been included as a specific defence in English law by the 2013 Defamation Act, which has created a new qualified privilege relating to peer-reviewed material in scientific or academic journals.

The French and English legal systems differ substantially. But this is a consequence of their cultures and histories. The common adherence of France and the UK to the Council of Europe and the application of the Convention on European Human Rights in both jurisdictions should, over time, erase the notable differences between the legal cultures. The way the European Court of Human Rights enforces privacy protection through Article 8 of the Convention has increased the protection of this right in Britain. The enforcement by the European Court of Human Rights of the protection of journalistic sources has made France uphold the rights of journalists not to disclose their sources to the police.

As time passes, the rights enshrined in the Convention on European Human Rights should lead most European countries to a common, if not unique, approach to the protection of free speech and individual privacy, and redress for individuals whose reputation has been injured by the defamatory statements of others. ☒

© Dominique Mondoloni
www.indexoncensorship.org

Dominique Mondoloni is a lawyer based in Paris, and the author of the chapter on France in the International Libel and Privacy Handbook, edited by Charles Glasser

Cape crusader

43(2): 88/92 | DOI: 10.1177/0306422014534385

A former political prisoner turned South African national treasure who helped to draft the constitution, parliamentarian Ben Turok worries about the future as he steps down after four terms in parliament. He talks to **Natasha Joseph** about the huge changes he has witnessed

PROFESSOR BEN TUROK has just taken a step into at least semi-retirement, he's still a busy man. The 87-year-old veteran political activist (he was arrested with Nelson Mandela in 1956) and ANC parliamentarian has lived through some of the most turbulent moments in the nation's history, and so is in a good position to comment on the challenges for the next decade.

Like many South Africans, corruption worries Turok. "It is eating the soul out of the country," he tells me. But it's not his biggest concern as he prepares to leave parliament and concentrate instead on editing New Agenda, the policy journal he founded nearly 11 years ago. Instead, he wants to see real economic growth driven by expansionary economic policies. He's tired of conservatism and a country that worries more about what ratings agencies say than what needs to be done to "get the economy moving".

"This must be done with rigour, discipline, foresight and boldness." There's nothing stopping us, as far as he's concerned – he disagrees with his colleague, Trevor Manuel of the Planning Commission, who worries about South Africa's skills shortage. "I think we have enormous manpower resources and brains but they're not being properly utilised. We must crack the problem of growth and we must grow in an inclusive, developmental manner."

Education, too, needs more work. He spent some time in Mozambique and was struck by the fact that every school stayed open late, until about midnight, to accommodate adult learners. In the United Kingdom, universities open their doors to adults who want to learn after a long day at work. "Why not in South Africa? We don't take education seriously. There's a far more rigorous attitude needed for training, teaching and learning. We've got to get serious. We need radical, strong solutions."

Turok has been discussing history recently, looking back to the 1940s and 50s to track the emergence of ANC policy. There is probably no one in the world who's better placed to comment on this subject: Turok is a policy wonk of the highest order; the man behind the socio-economic rights contained in South Africa's widely lauded constitution, and an ANC stalwart, he has no qualms about openly and eloquently criticising the party that's been his political home for decades. One of the most high-profile examples of this was his decision to speak out against the controversial secrecy bill, despite an ANC three-line whip. As Turok leaves parliament, there's little doubt that there's plenty

ABOVE: Veteran politician Ben Turok worries that not enough is being done to fight corruption in South Africa

more work to be done in strengthening and improving South Africa's very young democracy, but he is ready to focus his attentions elsewhere.

The son of Jewish immigrants from Latvia, Turok grew up in a fiercely political home. He and his parents moved to South Africa when he was about seven years old and his father, in particular, grew increasingly involved in anti-fascism after the end of the World War II in 1945. But, says Turok, his parents were "conventional" in terms of race, certainly in South African terms. "My parents," he says wryly, "were not revolutionaries at all." As an engineer-

ing student at the University of Cape Town (UCT), Turok started reading Marx and got involved with the Student Socialist Party. Eventually, he became the "broadly left-wing" organisation's chairperson. On the weekends, he would visit townships around Cape Town to sell copies of The Guardian. Still, he didn't consider himself truly politicised until he completed his studies at UCT and travelled to neighbouring Rhodesia (now Zimbabwe) to produce articles as a land surveyor.

"I had to live with farmers. On Sundays they would have neighbours round to chat and drink beer. I had African workers, →

from Nyasaland, and occasionally I had problems with the chief. The farmers were very clear about what they thought I should do – take [the workers] into the bush and beat the hell out of them."

He would listen, horrified, as the farmers boasted about "shooting Africans". They would even discuss the merits of different bullet calibres, suggesting to each other that it was better to use "a.22, not a.303, because then you wound, not kill". The experience hardened and, in many ways, defined the young Turok. "I was very angry."

He returned to South Africa and got involved in local politics. He was approached to help set up the Africa Club, a discussion

It was amazing under Madiba, there was a high quality of debate. There was so much change on the agenda and so many battles to be fought

and debate forum, and found premises for the organisation in Loop Street in Cape Town's city centre. Immediately, he says, the notorious and feared police Special Branch moved in, setting up outside the premises and jotting down the numberplates of those who were attending Africa Club sessions. "They didn't hide themselves."

In December 1952 (he thinks; for a man so well-versed in policy, able to home in on crucial details about complex economic issues, Turok admits he's "not very good with the dates"), Turok went to the UK for a year of post-graduate studies at London's Regent Street Polytechnic (now the University of Westminster). During his time there, he organised a festival for radical youth that drew people from around the world, among them 30 South Africans, including ANC leader Oliver Tambo. He also kept in touch with the woman who had succeeded

him as the secretary for the Modern Youth Society in Cape Town, Mary Butcher. She would later become his wife. He chuckles as he recalls how their relationship grew from attending political meetings together. "You know how that goes," he says – and cites other famous South African political couples, including Joe Slovo and Ruth First, Ahmed Kathrada and Barbara Hogan, and President Jacob Zuma and his former wife, the African Union commission chairperson Nkosana Dlamini-Zuma, to illustrate his point.

By the time Turok returned from the UK, the formalised apartheid system was about five years old. He and Mary could not join the ANC, as it was a blacks-only organisation. Instead, he became a member of the Congress of Democrats and, in 1955, became its secretary in the then Cape western region. He was a full-time organiser for the Congress of the People, held in Kliptown in Soweto in 1955. Here, the Freedom Charter was declared and adopted – a crucial document for the opponents of apartheid and, in some ways, a precursor to the country's constitution adopted in 1996.

Turok's political activites put him on a collision course with the apartheid government. Things, as he puts it, "got rougher and rougher". He was arrested and charged with treason in 1956 alongside Nelson Mandela, Tambo, First, Kathrada, Helen Joseph, Walter Sisulu, Duma Nokwe and others. Initially, 156 people were charged. Charges against Turok were withdrawn in 1958 and the entire treason trial, as it became known, ended in 1961 with "not guilty" verdicts for the remaining defendants. Both Turok and his wife were issued with banning orders by the apartheid government restricting their movement, but this didn't stop their political activities: in 1957 he started his first stint as a politician, representing black Africans in the Western Cape on the Cape Provincial Council.

In 1962, Turok was convicted under the Explosives Act and spent three years in prison. He eluded house arrest after serving his sentence, fled to Tanzania via Botswana and eventually moved his family – he and Mary had three sons – to Britain where he served on the faculty of the Open University.

But in 1990, it was time to come home. Turok tuned into the BBC and listened to South Africa's then President FW de Klerk announcing to parliament that the ANC and other political organisations were being unbanned. When Mary came home that afternoon, he announced that they were returning to South Africa. "She said OK," he reports, and two days later the couple flew into Johannesburg's Jan Smuts International Airport. Their sons, he says, "thought we were crazy". So did the security police who met them in Johannesburg and demanded to know why they were in the country. "Because De Klerk says we can come back," Turok declared. Eventually, the Turoks were allowed a week in Cape Town to visit Ben's brother.

Turok has served under four presidents as an ANC MP. He is a long-standing member of parliament's committees on finance, trade and industry, putting his policy nous to good work. The first parliament, assembled under Mandela after his inauguration in 1994, was "quite a shock to the system".

"It was amazing under Madiba, there was a high quality of debate and a mature, competent group of ministers. There was so much change on the agenda and so many battles to be fought."

For a man who's done so much in different guises over nearly an entire lifetime, it's hard to pinpoint his greatest success. But Turok is proudest of his contribution to the constitution, which started while he was still in exile and read a document compiled by the ANC called "constitutional guidelines". It included a bill of rights, but Turok noticed that there were no economic or even socio-economic rights contained in it. There was a similar absence in the first draft of what was to become the constitution of the Republic of South Africa. "I

ABOVE: South Africa's parliament in Cape Town

thought it was inadequate," says Turok, who had studied constitutional trends in the UK and Europe and knew there was a serious debate under way there to build a second level of socio-economic rights into the country's constitutions. He took his concerns to Mandela's legal advisor, Fink Haysom, during a meeting at the presidential guesthouse in Cape Town, Tuynhuys. Haysom was willing to listen – but Turok decided that he needed more evidence to bolster his case. He had a friend in London courier through 17 different documents →

→ that related to these rights and their place in constitutions, which he passed on to Haysom. After a couple of weeks, the lawyer came back to him and said "We'll do something about it." The government did, indeed, enshrining such values as the right to access to housing in the constitution – but it also built in limitation clauses that compelled the government to provide housing and other necessities only within its available resources. The rather liberal application of these clauses, Turok argues today, is behind such problems as South Africa's vast housing backlog. In late 2013, then Human Settlements Minister Tokyo Sexwale placed the backlog at around 2.1 million units – that's an estimated 12 million people without formal housing.

Turok is proudest of his contribution to the constitution, which started while he was still in exile

Turok says this involvement in the constitution is something he has no qualms boasting about: "And now I'm boasting to you!" On the eve of Turok's retirement from parliament, South Africa's political waters are turbulent. The country's public protector, Thuli Madonsela, has released a report into government spending on President Zuma's private home in Nkandla, KwaZulu-Natal. The ANC had recently faced harsh criticism for some of the names on its election candidate list. Among those on the list – although she later withdrew her candidature – was former Communications Minister Dina Pule, who was fired after parliament's ethics committee, led by Turok, found her guilty of gross misconduct. When her name appeared on the list, Turok was quoted as saying that he was disappointed by her inclusion. "I think that the ANC must uphold the best standards of ethical conduct," he told journalists.

Turok has plans for life after politics. From parliament, he may head over the road to his New Agenda offices or spend some time writing – "I love writing". He's already produced 21 books and his latest, With My Head Above The Parapet: An Insider Account Of The ANC In Power, was due out just days after our conversation. Retirement? That's for other people. Ben Turok still has far too much to do. ⊠

©Natasha Joseph
www.indexoncensorship.org

Natasha Joseph is news editor at City Press, Johannesburg

Syria's inside track

43(2): 93/95 | DOI: 10.1177/0306422014535688

Few journalists can reach the remote regions of Syria. Instead, thousands of citizens are helping get the news of the devastation out. **Vicky Baker** reports on an ambitious project to chart and verify countrywide citizen reports, social media updates and news articles

WHEN SYRIA TRACKER was launched in 2011 to crowdsource reports of deaths during the unfolding crisis, the volunteer team behind it expected the project to be over within a month. Similar efforts to cover the Haitian earthquake and Hurricane Sandy had all followed the same pattern: a short burst of intense activity, then the world moves on.

But three years in and with no end in sight, Syria Tracker's task to report news from the conflict has only grown. It is now believed to be one of the longest running crowdsourcing projects in the world, mapping over 4,000 geo-tagged verified eyewitness reports. It also incorporates large-scale data-mining techniques, so far scanning more than 160,000 news reports and 80 million social media updates. Maps (like the one created for Index on the next page) show the scale of citizen journalism happening in Syria, and its impact.

The Syrian conflict began in March 2011 when localised protests against President Bashar al-Assad's regime started to spread nationwide and, following military intervention, turned into an armed rebellion. The country soon descended into civil war, and both sides have been accused of serious human rights abuses. The death toll is now thought to have surpassed 100,000, with some sources putting the figure closer to 150,000 (including an estimated 11,000 children). Reporting the war is one of the world's most dangerous jobs. Aside being caught up in the violence, journalists also risk kidnapping. Many foreign news associations have withdrawn their reporters from the country. Citizen journalism has become a crucial way of informing the world about what's happening on the ground.

Taha Kass-Hout, a US-based social scientist and Syria Tracker's founder, says the work is relentless, "like a hurricane is happening every minute". Each member of the core team works around two to three hours a day on the project, somehow also holding down day jobs (as doctors, journalists, professors, PhD students and computer scientists). For the first two years, team members struggled to keep their identities secret and received constant threats, sent to their personal emails and Facebook pages. "We were hacked; the Syrian Electronic Army constantly tried to shut us down; but finally we 'came out' to show the project is manned by real people, not just a computer algorithm," says Kass-Hout.

Protecting the anonymity of their sources is, however, non-negotiable. The team →

THIS MAP PRESENTS DATA COLLECTED BY SYRIA TRACKER BETWEEN JUNE 2011 AND FEBRUARY 2014. IT SHOWS THE BALANCE OF NEWS ARTICLES AND CROWDSOURCED REPORTS FROM ACROSS SYRIA, HIGHLIGHTING AREAS WHERE TRADITIONAL MEDIA HAS LIMITED REACH. THE TOTAL OF NEWS REPORTS COMES FROM MINING OVER 2,000 SOURCES, INCLUDING PRO-REGIME OUTLETS. THE GRAPH PLOTS THE REPORTS OVER TIME; THE PEAK IN NEWS REPORTS IN 2013 CAME FROM A CHEMICAL ATTACK ON 22 AUGUST.

Syria is split into 14 governorates, including Damascus. This map shows 13, as the figures for Damascus have been combined with Rif Dimashq (the governorate of the Damascus region).

CROWDSOURCED REPORTS
100,280

NEWS ARTICLES
134,974

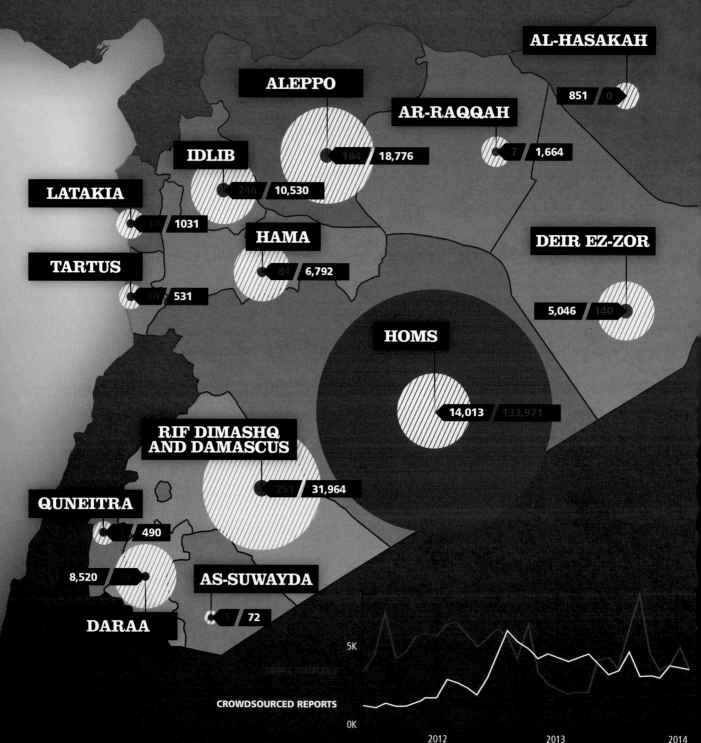

AL-HASAKAH
851 / 0

ALEPPO
184 / 18,776

AR-RAQQAH
7 / 1,664

IDLIB
246 / 10,530

LATAKIA
10 / 1031

HAMA
84 / 6,792

DEIR EZ-ZOR
5,046 / 140

TARTUS
10 / 531

HOMS
14,013 / 133,971

RIF DIMASHQ AND DAMASCUS
251 / 31,964

QUNEITRA
1 / 490

AS-SUWAYDA
0 / 72

DARAA
8,520 / 59

5K

NEWS ARTICLES

CROWDSOURCED REPORTS

0K

2012   2013   2014

Data from Syria Tracker, a Humanitarian Tracker project,
with assistance from Social Health Insights (socialhealthinsights.com)

Map design by Brett Evans Biedscheid (statetostate.co.uk)

→ immediately discounted the possibility of using text messages, with networks being monitored by the Syrian government. To power their project, they chose to use Ushahidi – open-source software for mapping and data-harvesting – which was developed after the 2008 Kenyan election and earlier this year helped with the public search for the missing Malaysian plane.

Only verified data is published – which equates to about 6 per cent of what they receive. Data-mined reports first go through an algorithm to look for patterns, before being analysed by members of the team. The crowdsourced reports are all manually checked – a process that can take several hours or several days. Any information that might identify the subjects is deleted; date stamps, landmarks and other nearby reports are correlated. Much of the video content is gruesome and of shaky quality, making the task even harder.

On the ground, the group has more than 600 citizen reporters. They aren't employees, but around 12 have worked with Syria Tracker constantly since 2011. "We've had sources that have worked with us for months, then suddenly the contact drops off. We never know if their group was dismantled, they've been killed or they're just missing."

The longevity of the project has also added complications. "Crowdsourcing projects often slow down because people get fed up that you aren't sharing anything back. So we make a point of engaging, sharing feedback, sending maps. Even if just to say, 'Hey, your info has been used here.'" Kass-Hout pinpoints their greatest achievement as when government agencies, NGOs and the media started to take their data seriously, publishing it alongside numbers from the UN.

But the "numbers game" is also frustrating, says Kass-Hout. "People query the number of deaths [currently over 100,200 documented by Syria Tracker]. They say the data is not representative, but it is clearly representative of something. Even rumour is valid. There is no such thing as bad data." One of the issues Syria Tracker has highlighted is the rising number of reports of women and children being attacked. "Even if you ignore the specific numbers, you can

Only verified data is published – about 6 per cent of what they receive

see that reports of female deaths have hit as much 18 per cent of the total deaths since the crisis began. And these are reports of rape and torture. This is not collateral damage."

Syria Tracker insists all it is trying to do is provide another tool for those attempting to piece together the full picture. "This is not a clinical trial," adds Kass-Hout. "We are telling a story, it's a living record." And so it continues. ☒

© Vicky Baker
www.indexoncensorship.org

Vicky Baker is deputy editor at Index on Censorship magazine

Index on Censorship
on the go

Find us in the app store today! A 30 day subscription costs just £1.79 and gives you access to 6 years of archived content.

- Search current issue or archive
- Share pages instantly via e-mail, Twitter, Facebook and other social networks
- Pinch or double-tap pages to zoom
- Use animated thumbnail view to flick through pages
- Swipe page edges to flip to next/previous page
- Sync any issue to your device for offline reading (WiFi)
- Tap links to take you to websites, email addresses, references, maps…
- Tap contents-page links to jump to a particular article

www.indexoncensorship.org/subscribe

Mapped out

43(2): 97/101 | DOI: 10.1177/0306422014536104

Maps bring power, and yet the people on the map have rarely had any say in how they are drawn. **Vicky Baker** explores how an Amerindian community in Guyana has drawn up its own maps using new digital tools, but has encountered death threats for doing so

"SOME PEOPLE ARE calling it the last land grab," says Ron James, of the battles to protect his people's ancestral territory, a rich mix of sweeping savannah, dense Amazonian rainforest and dramatic flat-top tepui mountains. James is one of the Wapichan, an indigenous population living in remote south-west Guyana, which has been fighting for the titles to its land. Amid increasing encroachment from miners and loggers, plus violent threats and intimidation, the Wapichan have responded with a protest tool of their own: mapping.

It all started with a visit in the mid-90s from then-president Cheddi Jagan who – perhaps unintentionally – set them the challenge to take map-making into their own hands. Conversation soon turned to the Wapichan's longstanding claim to 2.6 million hectares of land, which has been ongoing since before Guyana gained independence from Britain in 1966. The president put forward an ultimatum: the Wapichan needed to show how they use their land and why they demanded its control.

Guyana has long been a hotbed for territorial disputes. Even its international borders remain contested. Suriname, the former Dutch colony to the east, claims a southern chunk. Venezuela, to the west, wants an even larger portion, refusing to allow any border crossing as a result and leaving Guyana even more isolated from the rest of the world. "It must be a pretty claustrophobic experience being a map nerd in Guyana," wrote self-confessed map nerd Frank Jacobs in a New York Times piece about centuries of "cartographic aggression" in the region.

Internally, the fights are even fiercer. The country is 80 per cent covered in virgin rainforest; the little development it has hugs tightly to the coast and its muddy-brown stretch of Caribbean (so coloured for its proximity to the sediment-churning mouth of the Amazon). Guyana is a country the size of England with a population less than 800,000, and it is ripe for prospecting. Gold and diamonds are found here, as are bauxite, uranium and high-quality wood. Many concessions have government approval, but a large proportion of the mining and logging activity is illegal, often involving clandestine operations in the dead of night. Repercussions felt by the local community include deforestation, pollution – including mercury in the water, a byproduct from gold panning – and increased reports of rape, prostitution and human trafficking.

The Wapichan took President Jagan's challenge seriously. They went to the →

ABOVE: A Wapichan man watches the sunrise on the top of Savannah mountain, south-west Guyana

→ capital, Georgetown, to seek training and funding from the Amerindian Peoples' Association [APA], a national NGO rep-

Repercussions felt by the local community include deforestation and pollution – including mercury in the water, a byproduct from gold panning

resenting the nine indigenous peoples of Guyana. The then chief, Kokoi, told Index that the aim was to build on an initial

report lodged with the Amerindian Lands Commission in the 1960s. "Back then most of our chiefs did not know to read and write, so when I became chief, I kept reminding our peoples of the need to continue to pursue our land's legal recognition," he says.

The on-the-ground mapping took until 2000 to get under way. Much of it involved collecting GPS points, with the Wapichan setting out on expeditions by bike, motorbike or on foot – with some trips taking several days. Simple pen and paper played its role, too, as they called on members of the communities to join in, asking them to share picture of local sites that were important to them. Crucially, the communities were the ones deciding what was worthy of mapping. They mapped sacred sites, burial grounds, hunting areas, wildlife zones, rock carvings – and all were referenced in the Wapichan language.

"Amerindian land use is invisible to many," says Tom Griffiths, who works for the Forest Peoples Programme, an NGO that has provided assistance with the project. "People just don't see hunting, gathering and fishing as active use of the land. They only see it if you build a house or a bridge, or dig a hole." The Wapichan's map is concerned less with showing the way from A to B than with showing traditional occupation, negotiating inter-community politics and tracking illegal mining. "Baseline maps, based on surveys conducted decades ago by the British, with their 1:50,000 ratio, show limited detail and contain many errors," says Griffiths. "This led to confusion in official land use plans. Community boundaries are also misrepresented; and arguments over title boundaries abound."

The Wapichan's map took more than 10 years to produce and was compiled from over 30,000 GPS points. These points were then cross-referenced using satellite images to make sure everything lined up in the right place. In 2013, the US-based organisation Digital Democracy joined with the

Forest Peoples Programme to offer technical support after receiving a grant from the Knight Foundation to fund a new remote-access project. "[Digital mapping tools] aren't made with these end-users in mind," says Digital Democracy's director and founder Emily Jacobi. "These are people living in remote parts of the jungle, accessing the internet on their mobiles, with no broadband and very different needs. Which Silicon Valley investors are focusing on making apps for people with limited literacy and no bank accounts?"

This is where they step in to the bridge the gap. Digital Democracy has been working with the Wapichan to develop new mapping tools that can be used offline to suit their specific needs. As a starting point, they looked to OpenStreetMap, an open-source program that was used during the Haitian earthquake in 2010. During the crisis, the lack of decent maps of the country was inhibiting the response teams, so volunteers began tracing satellite images to create workable plans. Even when street signs were gone, aid workers and rescuers could still follow the contours of the map.

Since then, an in-browser tool called iD Editor has been devised to make OpenStreetMap easier to use, but it can only be used online, which, when traversing the depths of Guyana, is impossible. Digital Democracy has been working on an offline version that it is currently trialling. "The added bonus of an offline tool is data can be uploaded later. The community can choose when to share their information, and who to share it with, be it a legal group, an advocacy group or the government," says Jacobi. She believes it will be of benefit to other indigenous populations around the world, including Native American reservations in the United States.

The Wapichan are currently receiving funding from the UK's Department for International Development and Size of Wales, a Welsh initiative to protect an area of rainforest as big as the country. They have formed

a local NGO, too, called the South Central People's Development Association. These have helped fund an office – a small building on the open savannah, surrounded by mango trees – with solar panels, a satellite internet connection, three laptops and a printer. Jacobi says the introduction of technology needn't be seen as a threat to tradition. "So many [indigenous] people have been dealt this false dichotomy – where your choices are to assimilate so you don't get left behind, or be completely isolated," she says.

The idea is for the map to be dynamic and evolving, rather than static. The next stage involves monitoring all activity on the land and using the information in dialogue with national government agencies and to denounce deforestation and human rights abuses on global online platforms. Ron

Which Silicon Valley investors are focusing on making apps for people with limited literacy and no bank accounts?

James, Kokoi's son and the community's mapping technician, says he is looking forward to the next phase. "The monitoring team just came back with loads of information, in terms of how many illegal crossings are taking place from Brazilian ranchers coming in to rustle our cows and hunt in our land," he says. "We can upload their photos and information via the few internet points we have and, in a matter of days, our people can see, our leaders can see. Then we can make decisions, we can take it to the relevant authorities."

Of course, not everything important to the Wapichan makes the map. The areas rich in gold and diamonds, which the Wapichan know well, are not marked. "No map is ever neutral," says Peter Barber, head of map collections at the British Library →

→ and author of Magnificent Maps: Power, Propaganda and Art. "All are bound by conventions. All, for example, face north. Everything you put on it is hostage to fortune."

Barber also points out that it is a misconception to think that indigenous people have never been a part of the mapping process. Their knowledge has often been drawn on and many joined Western cartography expeditions as guides. However, their needs would not have been put first. "The West would get out of it what they wanted, without understanding the underlying values," says Barber. He references a chunk of beech bark, held in the British Library, which shows a hand-drawn route map drawn by indigenous people in Canada in the mid-1800s. It was collected by the British military and written beside it was a note, reminding young officers "how small an effort is needed to acquire that most useful art of military sketching, since even savages can make an intelligible plan".

Historically, the best-known example of an indigenous mapmaker is Tupaia, a Ra'aitean priest whom James Cook met in Tahiti. His charts were used by Cook to navigate Polynesia in the late 1700s and were incorporated (after being modified to meet Western mapping requirements) into his own maps, which formulated standard Western views of the region. Recent research has suggested that a similar set of circumstances occurred in around 1500, when the Portuguese reached the East Indies and shortly after, thanks to local navigators, found themselves able to chart the coast of Indo-China.

It's a leap backwards for indigenous people to have no say in official maps now, and a situation the Wapichan have been trying to correct – and not without problems. What happened to President Jagan, who first laid down the idea of proving the territory is in use? "He died," says Kokoi. "Now it's getting much more difficult. We are seen as extremists, and against development. My life has been threatened more than once."

But James says there are shoots of optimism, too: "Villages have presented detailed maps of their proposed land extensions to the government, complete with river and place names, and the government is now taking notice. The monitoring aspect of the project is very exciting and I can only hope that our leaders make maximum use of it."

Guyana once claimed it would be the world's first truly green economy. There is

We are seen as extremists, and against development. My life has been threatened more than once

still a long way to go and, 50 years since first lodging their claim, the Wapichan's work goes on. "Most people don't understand why land is important to us," says Kokoi. "We do not see the land as a commercial commodity, which can be sold for money. Our water sources are important for the entire world, but extractive activities are and will continue to destroy in the name of money and economic development. The lands are our supermarket, our university, our science labs, our libraries, our hospital, our recreational grounds, and, most importantly, they have spiritual value." ☒

©Vicky Baker
www.indexoncensorship.org

Vicky Baker is deputy editor of Index on Censorship magazine

PHOTOGRAPHS (ON PREVIOUS PAGE)

TOP LEFT: The Wapichan mapping project in progress
Credit: Tom Griffiths/Forest People Programme

TOP RIGHT: The Wapichan mapping project in progress
Credit: Tom Griffiths/Forest People Programme

BOTTOM: Rupununi savannah from the Kanuku mountains
Credit: Gregor MacLennan/Digital Democracy

When one door closes

43(2): 102/106 | DOI: 10.1177/0306422014535691

Historically it has been a bridge between Asia and Europe, but is Turkey now changing its position? **Kaya Genç** analyses the past and present

WHEN PICTURES OF Western-looking protestors fighting Turkish riot police appeared with increasing frequency in news bulletins, foreign observers wondered whether this was what a government closing its country to the outside world looked like. When the government blocked access to Twitter and YouTube days before local elections in March 2014, the question became more relevant and crucial. People all over the world watched and talked about Turkey, but those inside it lost some of the most crucial digital platforms they use to communicate their thoughts to those who watch them from afar.

What "outside world" means for a Western observer and, say, an Egyptian may not be the same thing. For the former, Turkey might already have been closing its borders to the outside world with its foreign policy over the last decade. For the latter, she may be doing just the opposite. Turkey is famously a bridge between continents; it shares borders with both Greece, a member of European Union, and Syria, one of the more chaotic Middle Eastern countries of our day. So the answer is as complicated as the question about openness. It may be that Turkey is becoming more open to a certain region (the Middle East and Asia), while not being as open to another (Europe). Yiğit Bulut, one of the most influential advisers of the Turkish prime minister, wrote an article in April saying the new world order

now consisted of "three main components: the American continent, the Turkey-Russia-Eurasia-Middle East line, and the China-India-Iran line." According to Bulut, Europe doesn't "exist" anymore and it is "impossible for it to be in the new balance of the world order". He wrote: "The American continent alone represents the Western power focus with its values and this representation will continue by getting stronger. There won't be any Europe in the new balance. Let me write clearly, in the new balance the new West is only America."

This seems to confirm the suspicion of numerous Western observers about a change of direction in Turkey's foreign policy. What the government understands as the West is the US, a close ally of Turkey since the foundation of the republic. According to this new understanding of foreign relations, Westernisation stands for the liberalisation of markets. In the eyes of the government, the French-rooted ideas of Enlightenment and Turkey's accession to the EU are no longer as important as they have been in the past decades. Speaking to CNN's Christiane Amanpour in 2012, Erdoğan complained of waiting "at the European Union's doorstep for 50 years" and not being allowed to become a member, despite the country's efforts. "No other country has experienced such a thing," he said. "We will be patient until a point."

If that point was reached through the country's continuing exclusion from the EU,

ABOVE: A Turkish passenger ferry sets sail across the Bosphorus Straits, which divides Europe and Asia

Credit: Osman Orsal/Reuters

then where does that leave us in regards to Turkey's openness to the outside world? The European Commission has been instrumental in encouraging the country to adopt reforms in the area of freedom of expression and civil liberties. It has also urged numerous Turkish governments to tackle human rights violations in the country. If Turkey turns its back on Europe and adopts a liberal approach only in the marketplace and not in the public sphere, the question is whether the right to protest and other public freedoms will suffer as a result.

To understand Turkey's relationship with the outside world, and discussions of the idea of "foreignness" and freedoms advocated by the West, it is important to look back a few years to see how it arrived at its current semi-closed position.

There was a time in Turkey when people treated foreign things with extreme suspicion. This was especially the case in the 1990s, my teenage years, when the country's nationalist ideology reached a feverish point. In the 15 years following the military coup of 1980, Turkish state ideology portrayed foreign things as responsible for the country's problems. For example, Turkey had battled for decades with the Kurdish question. According to the state discourse →

→ produced by the generals during the 1980s, Turkey's Kurds had struggled to preserve their language, identity and culture not because they wanted to secure those as their inalienable rights, but because foreigners somehow convinced them to do so. It was the same with civil society. NGOs, human rights groups and public intellectuals began severely criticising the state apparatus, not because they genuinely believed there was something wrong with its machinations, but because foreigners somehow convinced them to do so.

One of the most prevalent ideas of this discourse was that the people were not "ready for democracy". The public was portrayed as ignorant, unenlightened and lack-

At Istanbul's Italian embassy, anti-foreign protesters destroyed massive amounts of pasta to make their point

ing in sophistication. As Karl Marx famously wrote in The 18th Brumaire of Louis Napoleon: "They cannot represent themselves. They must be represented." Another argument was that those who found this discourse elitist and anti-democratic felt that way because foreigners somehow convinced them to think that way.

According to the militarist discourse, it was the British and Americans in particular who used their financial and ideological influence to bring dangerous ideas inside the country's borders. And following from that, the state could stop the flow of ideas if it really wanted to. A wave of anti-West protests, funded by the state, started taking place on streets. Foreign ideas were portrayed as dangerous for the country's security and unity. In the wake of a political crisis with Italy over the deportation process of the Kurdish leader Abdullah

Öcalan, state-affiliated groups kickstarted rallies against Italians, whom they accused of protecting Kurdish terrorists. In front of the Italian embassy in Istanbul, anti-foreign protesters destroyed massive amounts of pasta to make their point. When two Leeds fans were killed by Turkish fans in Istanbul in 2000 (a few metres away from the now famous Gezi Park, the location of last year's protests), a jingoistic newspaper did little to conceal its delight. It boasted about how Turks had defeated the English in the stadium (the score was two-nil) and out in the street.

Killing foreigners was clearly felt to be OK, since, according to the state discourse, dark forces like George Soros and his Open Society Foundation were secretly plotting against the government under the guise of democracy, human rights and individual freedoms. It was all doublespeak; it suggested that demanding freedom was equal to demanding slavery and that the ostensibly progressive ideas of liberals would bring the country back to the middle ages.

NGOs like Greenpeace, Helsinki Citizens' Assembly and Amnesty International were seen as suspect and their representatives were portrayed as puppets in the pay of shadowy power centres from the West. Writers with cosmopolitan views were handpicked and made scapegoats of all that went wrong in the country. Similar traitors had existed during Turkey's war of independence in the 20th century and the revolutionary elite had severely punished them. Why not set the clocks back a few decades and do the same to those foreign agents? This was achieved through a political campaign orchestrated by mainstream national newspapers. Those who had been targeted either had to flee the country, or live with police protection so as not to be assassinated by counter-guerilla forces.

The campaign to close Turkey to the outside world took a big hit in 1999, when a massive earthquake rocked the country. The state infamously refused blood aid from the Greek government. The argument was that the purity of the Turkish blood could be contaminated. It was the government's duty to preserve the purity of the race. The famous maxim of the day was grammatically simple: "The Turk has no other friend but the Turk." Foreigners, be they Greeks or Arabs, were natural enemies.

According to the state discourse at the time, the most dangerous idea Turkey could have was democracy, which was a Greek concept anyway. Turks were simply not ready for it, as they had not been during the previous eight decades. If the country wanted to survive in its current form, it was crucial that an enlightened elite, and not ignorant masses, continued ruling it.

This idea changed dramatically when the representatives of the closed-Turkey discourse lost the general elections in 2002, but not quite the way Turkey-watchers and liberals had expected. According to many, the shift of power from left- and right-wing nationalists to conservative democrats (AKP) would bring about the country's integration with the Western world. The problem with this analysis was that it ignored the anti-Orientalist element in the new government's discourse. Turkey's conservative democrats were different from other conservative parties in the West, in that they built their discourse on a critique of what they had seen as the imposition of an Orientalist-Westernising discourse on the country during the 20th century. Among their political aims was to reach a post-nationalist era.

When it became clear during the last five years that the conservative-democrat government's idea of openness included openness to the Eastern world, the debate took a different turn. When, following a Davos meeting in 2009, Erdogan accused Israel of committing crimes against humanity in the West Bank, The Guardian reported how he was greeted with "cheering crowds and mass adulation" in Cairo. While Turkey's interest in the Palestinian cause was welcomed in some quarters, it was watched with suspicion in others. Turkey wanted to portray itself as a model democracy in the Middle East, arguing that its conservative-democratic outlook could be a magic formula for countries divided between cultures of a Ba'ath-style secularism and radical Islamism. But the model country argument was problematic for many secularists at home, who advised the government to mind its own business and pay more attention to national matters.

According to its domestic critics, the key reason why the government wanted to be open to the outside world was related to

For conservative-democrats Turkey is better off doing business in Asian and African countries where it has historical ties

Islam and the idea of a caliphate. This institution from Ottoman times gave the power of representation of all Muslims to the Ottoman Sultan and his office in Istanbul. After the Ottomans defeated the Arabs and started controlling the Arabian peninsula in the 16th century, the title of Caliph was transferred to Ottoman rulers and symbols of the Caliphate were moved to Istanbul. Towards the late 18th century, Ottoman sultans started using the Caliph title in international affairs and the title made Istanbul the centre of all Muslim people. Until it was abolished in 1924, the title gave Ottomans extra-territorial influence over all Islamic lands. The new republic's secular politics, on the other hand, were based on self-sufficiency, and territorial and cultural independence.

So there have been different approaches, and motivations, to openness in Turkey's →

→ political culture. For nationalists, Turkey is better off when it is self-sufficient. It has plenty of resources and it does not need Europe, the US, or business ventures in Africa, to survive. In contrast, for liberals, Turkey is better off as a partner of Europe and a full EU member. Commerce and cultural integration with European partners are good things for the country and are a natural continuation of the Westernising vision of its founders. For conservative-democrats Turkey is better off doing business in Asian and African countries where it has long-held historical ties.

The government's ruthless response to environmental protesters in 2013 unsettled this picture further. According to Turkish officials, the protests were partly provoked by power centres outside Turkey. When the government looked for those responsible in leaking wiretaps about Turkish politicians on Twitter and YouTube, the category of "outside world" provided an useful answer. But the clampdown on social media that began in March was partly paradoxical, as it came from politicians who are themselves very active on those platforms. The prime minister has more than four million followers on Twitter, who heard nothing from him there for two weeks after a ban was imposed on that website. It seemed as if, in the harsh election atmosphere of Turkey, the international ambitions of the government were paused. Entrepreneurial and political openness to the outside world, whether it involved Europeans or Muslims, was put on hold because of national concerns.

During the last couple of years liberals and secularists, who have demanded openness to the Western world, have felt disappointed by what they identify as a decrease in Turkey's willingness to adopt EU reforms. Now it may be the conservatives' turn to criticise the government because of its loss of interest in the outside world. If Turkey wants to play an influential role beyond its borders (in the Middle

East as well as in Europe, where millions of Turks live), it will need to remember the responsibilities that come with being more open to the outside world. ☒

© Kaya Genç
www.indexoncensorship.org

Kaya Genç is a novelist and journalist, based in Istanbul, and has translated 10 books into Turkish. He was named as one of Turkish literature's top 20 writers under 40. He tweets @kayagenc

LA story

43(2): 107/110 | DOI: 10.1177/0306422014536303

As Los Angeles prepares for the 30th anniversary of its Olympics, it is embracing a new attitude to art and graffiti. **Ed Fuentes** reports

FOR OVER A decade, murals in Los Angeles were banned. Urban walls that once told the stories of its communities – Mexican-American, African-American, Asian, Jewish – were neglected or whitewashed over, as a litigation battle played out between advertising companies and city authorities.

It was only late last year when the ban was finally lifted, following two years spent drafting new regulations on murals, with discussions between the city, artists and cultural administrators. During the ceremonial sign-off inside City Hall, Isabel Rojas-Williams, executive director of the Mural Conservancy of Los Angeles, who organised many public meetings between the city and muralists, lifted the proclamation over her head in victory.

"Under the new policy, graffiti will be protected and share the same rights as traditional murals," says Pilar Castillo, archivist for the Social Public Art and Resource Center (SPARC). "Unfortunately, it does nothing to help change the public perception of graffiti as mere vandalism. And the fact remains: graffiti is in its essence an art form that needs no permission to roam the streets." SPARC was founded after initial murals from the Citywide Mural Programme – including depictions of residents' clashing with the police – were censored in its first year.

Los Angeles was once known as the mural capital of the world. In the 1960s and early 1970s, large-scale street paintings flourished. Mexican artists David Siqueiros, José Clemente Orozco and Diego Rivera, made up *Los Tres Grandes*, the big three, who moved murals away from decorative illustration, adding social and political messages. California's avant-garde art circles welcomed the trio and a new generation of muralists, including Judith Baca, Kent Twitchell and Alonzo Davis, tapped into civil rights themes and multiculturalism.

"Los Angeles once had some 1,500 or more murals," says mural historian James Prigoff. "But the title of 'mural capital' has long since moved to Philadelphia, which has more than 3,000 major murals to their credit." What happened? Billboard advertising. In the 1980s, "super graphics" sprung up around LA – large painted signs on walls and digital banners hanging across multiple floors of high-rise buildings, all designed to catch the eyes of commuters. The general public protested against the ugliness and clutter and, in 1986, the city responded by adopting a "sign code" to regulate outdoor graphics. Certain murals were allowed, they concluded, if they were deemed a "fine art mural" and as long as text did not exceed three per cent of the composition.

Media companies sued, demanding that advertising signs be given the same free-speech protection as murals. Two →

ABOVE: Frank Romero's Going to the Olympics mural was restored in 2013 after vandals had tagged it

decades of legal battles ensued and, in 2002, the court ruled that a general ban be imposed on outdoor advertising until a resolution was found. The ban even extended to private property, but did not apply to city, county, state and federal buildings, or sites operated by the Los Angeles Unified School District and Metro, which commissioned murals freely during the moratorium.

The city has continually struggled with its contradictory messages on public art. Where do the boundaries between advertising and art lie? What constitutes a fine art mural? What to do with artists, such as Shepard Fairey and Barbara Kruger, whose work is text heavy as a post-modern response to the visual linguistics of advertising? Is whitewashing censorship?

Many people lump all street artists together – from muralists to graffiti artists and taggers. But an insider knows it is a scene with many different strands. In their fight to revive the city's reputation for murals, many divergent artists and subcultures banded together. Traditional muralists, empathic to suppressed voices, welcomed graffiti and street artists, and together they rallied the city to change the policy. It was testy at first, especially since taggers constantly took their spray cans to vintage murals.

The reputation of street art was bolstered enormously by Art in the Streets, a 2011 exhibition by the Los Angeles Museum of Contemporary Art. It gave aerosol new credibility and inspired new, large-scale street art in the downtown Los Angeles Arts District, by artists including JR, Dabs and Myla, INSA, Shepard Fairey, How and Nosm. The drafting of the mural ordinance began as the exhibition ended, and by the time it was passed, all forms of murals were recognised by the city – as long as artists registered them with the city and paid a $60 application fee. The works also cannot contain a commercial message and must remain for at least two years, as part of the city's continuing battle to keep tabs on advertising. The rules apply to public areas with residential areas having to "opt in" if they want artworks on their walls and homes.

"Within the new ordinance, muralists are required to involve the communities in which the works will be created," says Rojas-Williams. "Tagging is also reduced in this way. When communities are involved in the creative process there is a good deal less desire to vandalise or censure." Muralists of different styles now plan to work together on pieces around the city. "Graffiti artists will continue to collaborate with pioneer muralists and to take the time to hone their skills, instead of looking over their shoulders, afraid of prison or fine threats," says Rojas-Williams. In LA, graffiti is also often associated with gang culture. The police often stopped artists with

Media companies sued the city, demanding that advertising signs be given the same free-speech protection as murals

spray cans – including those that had no gang connections and who had permission from a property owner.

But the new policy – which was inspired by a similar ordinance in Portland, Oregon – has not been without its problems. The first challenge came in January, when, without proper permits, the LA Freewalls project – which controversially brokers deals between businesses and street artists – installed three street-art works in downtown Los Angeles to promote a beer, a shoe company and a band's new album. The works were criticised by the community, saying they violated the spirit of the new murals' policy.

Los Angeles is now preparing for the 30th anniversary of the series of celebrated murals produced along the 101 Freeway for the 1984 Summer Olympic Games. In the last few years the murals have been beleaguered by vandals, weather damage and nearby →

ABOVE: Italian street artist Blu was commissioned by the Museum of Contemporary Art in 2010 to create this piece for their Arts in the Street festival, only for the museum to have it whitewashed on completion due to the image's strong political message

→ constriction work, some have been damaged beyond repair but those that have been restored include artist Frank Romero's vibrant depiction of a traffic jam, Going to the Olympics. The Mural Conservancy of Los Angeles has also recently announced it will be restoring its first graffiti-style work: They Claim I'm a Criminal by Man One at the Southern California Library.

"Will Los Angeles reclaim its title as mural capital of the world?" asked a panel discussion of the same name at the LA Art Show in January. Locals think the city is well on its way to regaining its position. ☒

©Ed Fuentes
www.indexoncensorship.org

Ed Fuentes is a writer, photographer and muralist, based in Los Angeles. He tweets @ viewfromaloft

Secrets and lives

43(2): 111/114 | DOI: 10.1177/0306422014537945

Much has been written about the nuclear scientists of Los Alamos, but very little about the wives of those scientists and the secrecy that they had to live with. Novelist **TaraShea Nesbit** spent three years collecting personal stories about the families

IN THE SPRING of 1943, young women from Europe and America were told by their husbands they were moving to the US southwest, but where, exactly, the men could not say. Unbeknown to these wives, their husbands were developing the first atomic bombs.

Eleanor Jette's husband came home from work one day and asked: "How'd you like to move to the southwest?" She had confidence she could, with some spy work, decode the location. Another wife went to the university library to do some research on the area and saw that the New Mexico travel books had been previously checked out by two other scientists who has recently disappeared for war work. Their new lives were part of a series of suspicions, followed by guesses.

Many women came to Los Alamos by train, without their husbands, and were instructed to get off at the Lamy station. Someone in Lamy would drive them the 30 minutes to Santa Fe, where they met Dorothy McKibben, at 109 East Palace. She gave them a map, took their fingerprints, instructed them to board a military bus, and onward they went another hour up switchbacks, before they arrived at a gate with a barbed wire fence and a Keep Out sign.

Though the town was supposed to be a secret, the black smoke rising from the coal chimneys gave it away. It was always under construction to accommodate for growth, from a few families to a few thousand. Jette described the appearance "as raw as a new scar". When people in Santa Fe grew suspicious, or curious, Robert Oppenheimer, who brought the best minds in physics together at Los Alamos to work on the atomic bomb, asked one wife to go try to spread a rumor in Santa Fe that would throw the residents off-course. "Do you ever wonder what we are building up there?" one wife would say. And when a stranger said yes, perhaps she could say they were building a rocket ship.

Even if they had a lifetime of navigating gossip, the women found this new location, high on a mesa in New Mexico, in a town that, on paper, didn't even exist, created new tensions. The military's presence, with their guns, their Dobermans, and their requests that IDs be carried at all times, reminded one of the wives, Laura Fermi, of the very reason she had left Italy.

Once they had been dancers in the Chicago ballet, or doctoral students at Ivy League colleges, and now they were told to make dinners with what little wilted produce was available at the commissary and on a stove that often did not function. The initial surprise, and perhaps sense of adventure, of going to some unknown →

ABOVE: Women and families living in Los Alamos knew little about the Manhattan Project to create the atomic bomb

→ location in the west soon wore off. Where once they took baths, they were now instructed to take brief showers in stalls lined with zinc, although water shortages often prevented them from showering at all. The women were asked to work and if they refused they were accused of being disloyal

Women attempted to pull pieces of information together to work out what their husbands were up to in the lab

to their country. Wives who had PhDs in chemistry were asked to take typing tests. Their husbands were away 12 hours a day at the lab, and when they arrived home and their wives asked: "How was your day?" these scientists could not say. The husbands could no longer turn to their wives for support. Women grew jealous of the female scientists, who were able to be their confidants. At least one woman said she could not take

it any longer and went to Reno for a divorce.

Because their husbands could tell them nothing, and the military posters threatened them for discussing anything war-related, the women created their own sources of information. The women attempted to pull pieces of information together to work out what their husbands were up to in the lab. Husbands urged their wives to keep their speculations to themselves, but when some wives were sunbathing with their friends at Frijoles Canyon, they discussed if their husbands were building some kind of super bomb. Martha suggested a weapon that could draw its energy from the sun. Jette did not think so and shared that every time she made a guess her husband Eric hooted: "He hoots so loud it makes me think I may be right." Husbands told their wives that their guesses were completely incorrect, but said not to tell anyone about their ideas.

And one weekend in July, Fermi recalled, "Nobody who was anybody was left in Los Alamos, wives excepted, of course". On 15 July, a woman physicist told Fermi that she, her husband and a few others were driving to the Sandia Mountains, near Albuquerque, to camp. She said that if the wives were able to stay awake, they might see something. What that something was, Fermi did not know. At least one husband told his wife that if she stayed up late she, too, might see something. The next morning the grapevine reported that a hospital patient, who had been unable to sleep, had seen, near dawn, a strange light. Later that evening, the scientists returned, and Fermi recalls that Enrico, a bit sunburned, "went to bed without a word". The word "Trinity" was in the air, Fermi said, and though her husband Enrico loved to drive, he announced that he no longer felt able to do so.

One husband told his wife to leave for the weekend. Such clearance was not easy to come by, one could rarely be granted permission to leave the barbed-wired, fenced-in town. To get in, they needed a security clearance, and once inside, they needed a pass to leave. But if your parent died, you might be allowed to leave. And so one wife told the military that her father was on his deathbed. But he was not dying. Her husband gave her the code phrase: "The cat cried all night when you left." When he wrote to her – and their mail was censored – and said that phrase, she knew it was safe to return. Why, she wondered, did other husbands not do the same? But most women did not leave that weekend. The local paper reported a bright light and speculated it was an ammunitions storage facility blowing up. In actuality, what they had seen was the Trinity Test, the test before bombs were detonated in Japan, at the White Sands Missile Range, between Las Cruces and Alamogordo in New Mexico.

Once the bombs were detonated on civilians in Japan, the town's secret was out, and the women's responses were conflicted. Fermi was disturbed to learn she and her husband had contributed to building the bombs that destroyed Hiroshima and Nagasaki. But her feeling was not the pervading one in town; she locked herself in the bathroom so that

ABOVE: Scientists at Los Alamos moved their families from around the US and Europe to be close to them

others would not see her tears. She recalls: "I have never lost the sense of helplessness I felt so strongly that day, August 6, 1945." Where

Once the bombs were detonated in Japan, the town's secret was out, and the women's responses were conflicted

other wives hoped this bomb would end war, another wife Phyllis Fisher pondered how mutual support and understanding could ever be taught when people were killing one another.

Some wives thought Los Alamos had caused the war to end six months early and saved the lives of soldiers. Jette, who →

→ remained in the town after the war, felt that the name Los Alamos, if not the cause for peace, would be the cause of scorn. She says she prayed for peace after World War II, "lest the name of Los Alamos live in infamy forever". Fisher called her time there two "very crucial and upsetting years". Her sense of culpability can be seen in her memoir, Los Alamos Experience, which she addresses to the "Little Lady of Hiroshima": "I wanted to tell you [little lady of Hiroshima] that, as an American woman, I grieved with you. I wanted to say, 'I'm sorry'."

They were years of fear heightened by mysteries and secrets. They were years, in many ways, not unlike the present. ☒

©TaraShea Nesbit
www.indexoncensorship.org

TaraShea Nesbit teaches at the University of Denver, and her latest book is The Wives of Los Alamos (Bloomsbury). She tweets @t_nesbit

A good book will keep you fascinated for days. A good bookshop for your whole life.

Waterstones

ABOVE: A demonstrator, draped in a Brazilian flag, during the riots in Rio de Janeiro, June 2013

Marching on

43(2): 116/120 | DOI: 10.1177/0306422014534583

Brazil's pre-World Cup riots took the nation, and the world, by surprise, bringing out a cross-section of protesters on to the streets to call for change. But did that change happen?
Nicole Mezzasalma reports

WHEN A GROUP of disgruntled right-wing activists announced a protest in São Paulo in March, there were fears it could escalate into a replay of the full-scale riots the year before. This year's Marcha da Família (Family March) may have had very different aims to the riots – calling for the military to overthrow the president, rather than an improvement of public services – but the fuse for street action had been lit. Prescient in everyone's minds was a demonstration of the same name 50 years earlier that drew in over 100,000 supporters and caused a coup that led to a 21-year dictatorship.

Yet, despite over 2,100 confirmations on a Facebook event page, this year's Marcha da Família went out with a fizzle rather than a bang, attracting around 700 demonstrators in São Paulo and a few more at satellite protests nationwide. Domestic news coverage was minimal; internationally, it didn't even register. No one expected another coup but it was certainly tamer than predicted.

Aside from last June's riots and the Marcha da Família of 1964, Brazil is not a nation prone to protest. Pots are banged in the plaza on a regular basis in Argentina; in Bolivia, people band together to march on the presidential palace. In contrast, Brazilians rarely take →

→ to the streets to voice their problems. They are quick to remind people that their country was not born from a bloody revolution.

Hence the shock felt, both domestically and internationally, from last year's large-scale demonstrations, when hundreds of thousands of discontented people poured on to the streets. Even major news organisations were caught off-guard. "The news team here had never covered large-scale national protests. We had to import all kinds of protective riot gear and helmets so we could go out in the field," said a news agency journalist in Rio.

The initial impetus for the June riots was outrage at a rise in bus fares, but this soon snowballed. Discontent spread nationwide and drew in more issues: corruption, the cost of hosting the FIFA World Cup, the lack of investment in health and education. Demonstrations became riots when the heavy-

Brazil is not a nation prone to protest. Brazilians rarely take to the streets to voice problems

handed approach of police towards the until-then-peaceful events triggered a wave of support, which culminated in an estimated two million Brazilians joining protests across more than 100 cities.

International observers might not have realised how out of character this was for Brazilians, but the scale of the events was certainly surprising given that the country had been riding a wave of economic progress. President Dilma Rousseff's approval ratings back then were high (63 per cent of the population rated the government as good or excellent in March 2013). But did the action – and all the worldwide headlines – have any effect?

Political scientist and Amnesty International human rights adviser Mauricio Santoro said the June protests achieved some immediate results: "The bus fare rises

that originally triggered the movement were cancelled in Rio and São Paulo, and while they have since risen once more in Rio, the fares in São Paulo remain the same." The impact of the demonstrations also affected the federal sphere. "As well as the local gains, nationally the protests resulted in the approval of certain laws and the repeal of others that were heavily criticised," said Santoro. This included a proposed amendment to the constitution that aimed to reduce the powers of the Brazilian Prosecution Service, widely viewed as a way to prevent the government from taking firm action to curb corruption, particularly in the political arena. The proposal was rejected by federal MPs as a direct result of protests.

However, he warned that the changes have been very small and certainly much less significant than protesters wanted. "The protests happened not only because of the rise in bus fares. They were also about the public transport service's lack of quality and infrastructure." Buses in the main Brazilian cities are regularly overcrowded, accidents due to reckless driving are common, and they are constantly the target of thieves and other criminals. "And, to this day, none of these structural problems have been resolved or investigated," Santoro said.

A good example of this is the investigation into the contracts to operate bus lines in Rio de Janeiro, originally tendered in 2010 and plagued with complaints ever since. As a consequence of last year's protests, in August the city council opened a CPI (comissão parlamentar de inquérito, or parliamentary inquiry commission) to delve into the lack of transparency surrounding the contracts and fare structures. But little more than a month later, Rio's courts suspended the commission's work after a group of councillors claimed that not all political parties were equally represented in it. Legal battles are still being fought to restore it.

Sociologist and researcher Aline Khoury co-wrote an article for Economic & Political

Weekly analysing the protests, concluding that while the lasting effects would be hard to judge, the events had succeeded in awakening Brazilians from a long-term political lethargy. "The bus fare complaints that sparked the whole movement ultimately did not achieve their goals, as prices have gone up since then and the bus operators' contracts were not reviewed or scrutinised. There have been more subtle political gains, however, and it is easier to study them today than it was back then," she said.

"We saw that the upper-middle class, which had no direct interest in the bus fare issue and in general was averse to public demonstrations – they depend less on public policy as they can afford private healthcare and education, for example – took to the public spaces and rubbed shoulders with the lower classes for the first time ever."

The downside of their presence in the protests, Khoury added, was the fragmentation of ideas, which changed the general democratic focus of the original movement into several marches defending the interests of particular groups. Doctors, for example, protested against the arrival en masse of Cuban medical practitioners as part of a federal plan to send them to underprivileged and underrepresented parts of the country that do not attract young health professionals.

Professor David Samuels from the University of Minnesota's Department of Political Science specialises in Brazilian and Latin American politics and democratisation, and has a more cynical view of the protests' motivations and achievements. "I really don't think that these protests were society-wide – I believe they represent mainly urban upper-middle class people together with assorted middle-class protesters. I don't see a unifying theme for the demonstrations, so the idea that this is a 'soft revolution' seems a little misguided to me," he said. "In the case of Egypt, Turkey or, more recently, the Ukraine, there has been a clear target – toppling the government – and what is unusual about the events in Brazil is that they weren't even targeting Dilma or the [ruling Labour Party] PT. They kept highlighting that they were not partisan and that is an indication that they did not know what they wanted and that the movement was ephemeral. That is still my view today and now you hardly see any protests happening – you have strikes and smaller events, such as Occupy City Hall in Rio, but people are not universally discontent."

To Samuels, Brazilians display a level of disengagement with politics that is especially evident among the youth. He said: "Brazil is not unusual in that respect; young people perceive the world very clearly through Twitter and Facebook and it all looks pretty grim. To them, there is no real way of effect-

College students are easily mobilised, but long-term movement is much harder and there is no clear evidence of that in Brazil today

ing change through these channels." He said that the only real achievement [from the protests] was that, with the PT in power, it was still possible for people to protest. College and high-school students are easily mobilised, but to have a consistent long-term movement is much harder and there is no clear evidence of that in Brazil today.

Samuels predicts that protests during the World Cup and before the general elections in October will be, at best, sporadic as the upper-middle and middle classes will not want the country to be represented badly in the international media, while the lower classes will be happy to watch the football even without being able to get into the stadium due to the high ticket prices. "For a real revolution to happen people need a proper target – it happened during the →

→ dictatorship [of the 60s and 70s] and it happened when President Fernando Collor de Melo was impeached, when people rallied for several months until something was actually achieved," he added. "I think part of the problem with the recent protests in Brazil is that people say they are tired of corruption and impunity, but there is not enough political will to really end these problems. Only a small percentage of the population think corruption is an issue that should be higher up on the agenda – the majority just don't care."

Santoro holds a more optimistic view and believes the June 2013 protests were only the beginning of a larger mobilisation. "This October we will have the first elections in Brazil since the demonstrations took place and we will be able to see the true impact of the protests. The president's popularity has plunged since last year and while there has been some recovery, the consequences could still be seen in the poll. The same goes for the governors of Rio and São Paulo."

But Santoro says there have also been negative consequences to the increase in size and visibility of the demonstrations. "In June, three-quarters of Brazilians were pro-protests, but now just above 50 per cent of the population support the activities. This is due in great part to the increase in violence – the demonstrations have become more aggressive and police repression has been more pronounced. The results are that we don't know how big the protests during the World Cup will be, but I think we will certainly see people on the streets again."

Santoro said there is a direct correlation between government supporters and those who have positive feelings towards the World Cup. "The critical movement began well after Brazil's selection to host the event was announced, so the World Cup itself was not a trigger. Rather, it is an opportunity to showcase and vent general dissatisfaction. For example, traffic in Rio has worsened considerably in the last few months and it is bound to get even worse during the tournament, and people could protest against that. There could also be demonstrations because the changes have not gone far enough."

With the results of the protests in Brazil less tangible than those in Egypt or Turkey, it is hard to see what happened last year as a soft revolution. "The giant has woken," said the press, a reference to the commonly held opinion that Brazil used to be a country full of potential, but little will to realise that into tangible prosperity. Recent surveys indicate the percentage of the population that is pro-protests has fallen from 81 per cent to 52 per cent, and 42 per cent now declare themselves as altogether against the demonstrations. While the country may not be as completely disengaged from the political sphere as people believed, it looks as though last year's events were more a blip on the radar than a giant's awakening. ⊠

© Nicole Mezzasalma
www.indexoncensorship.org

Nicole Mezzasalma is a London-based Brazilian journalist

Free Speech Bites

Explore the development of free speech in **Free Speech Bites** a series of podcasts produced by Index in association with SAGE.

In each episode, celebrated philosophy writer Nigel Warburton (@PhilosophyBites) and guests explore the concept, why it matters and highlight individuals who advanced the idea of freedom of thought.

Timothy Garton Ash on his Free Speech Debate project, a forum for discussing global free speech standards in the digital age

DJ Taylor on George Orwell's nuanced attitude to free speech and his encounters with censorship

Denis McShane on the legacy of Enlightenment philosopher Tom Paine, author of The Rights of Man

Natalia Kaliada on the difficulty of creating art in Europe's last dictatorship

Martin Rowson on humour, satire and offence

Irshad Manji on the clashes between religion and free speech

Zarganar on the importance of thinking and speaking freely, even under tyranny

Stephanie Merritt on how renaissance astronomer, mathematician and heretic Giordano Bruno inspired her bestselling "SJ Parris" series

Jonathan Dimbleby on the philosophy of John Stuart Mill and why free speech matters

Subscribe to the podcasts via iTunes & follow on Twitter @FreeSpeechBites

www.indexoncensorship.org/free-speech-bites-podcasts

SUPREME COURT'S D[E]
REFLECTS T[
'ROTTEN DEMOC[
WE HAVE COME
LIVE UNDER
#INDIA

ABOVE: An LGBT activist in New Delhi demonstrates against the India Supreme Court's re-criminalisation of gay sex

History revision

43(2): 122/126 | DOI: 10.1177/0306422014537155

Colonial laws often get blamed for repression of dissent, and for inequality in India, but why haven't they been changed in the 67 years since independence? **Saurav Datta** reports

"I AM A law-abiding citizen, and [go] strictly by the statute book," said Dina Nath Batra, who has achieved notoriety and fame in equal measure for his legal challenge to Penguin India and author Wendy Doniger that recently ended up with her books being pulped. Anyone who cherishes freedom of expression would describe Batra as a bully, and his tactics intimidatory, but would also be hard pressed to find even a smidgen of illegality in his actions. The reason is a set of provisions in India (Sections 153A, 298 and 295A of the Indian Penal Code – IPC) allowing people to seek legal redress on grounds of their religious or ethnic sentiments and sensibilities being offended. It also allows the government to ban and censor books, films and plays.

Much of the legal framework used to crack down on social liberalism and dissent in India harks back to the colonial era before independence, when the British administration attempted to impose Victorian values. The IPC was framed and brought into →

→ force in 1860 by the British colonial administration and includes provision to take action against threats of sedition, waging war against the state, and obscenity, among others.

It was hoped that India was ready to reform these archaic laws and there were moves towards change, but those moves have rolled back again. In 2009 the Delhi High Court decriminalised homosexuality, legislation that harked back to British colonial rule, and gay rights activists hailed the decision as a symbol of a new era. But in December 2013, the Supreme Court of India overturned the ruling.

In February 2009, the editor and publisher of The Statesman, a daily paper based in Calcutta, were dragged to court by a group of Muslims infuriated by their reprint-

Draconian colonial laws remain because of the way identity politics has played out in post-independence India

ing of an article from UK newspaper The Independent. The "offending" article was Johann Hari's Why Should I Respect These Oppressive Religions?, a trenchant criticism of the myths and beliefs of Christianity, Islam and Jewism. Before that, in April 1993, a university student, Nancy Jamshed Adajania, was charged under Section 153A by the Maharashtra government, apparently for authoring a "deeply offensive" article, Myth and Supermyth, which had created a furore in the legislature because the dominant Maratha community felt their idol Shivaji (a Hindu king of the Middle Ages) had been insulted. The Bombay High Court subsequently quashed the charges, holding them to be "distressing, misguided and misdirected", but this was after the publishers of the magazine that published the piece,

fearing the mob's ire, had beaten a hasty retreat and tendered a profuse apology.

Filmmaker Deepa Mehta's Fire (1998) looked at a lesbian relationship between a young Hindu bride and her sister-in-law. The film saw a severe backlash from the Sangh Parivar (the group of Hindu nationalist organisations associated with the Bharatiya Janata Party) and other assorted groups. Film sets were vandalised, screenings were halted, because it was considered to have subverted every strand of the "respectable sexuality" and patriarchal control which are considered inalienable parts of Adarsh Bharatiya culture and "essential" to the nationalist discourse.

A common reaction to discussions of why these laws are in place is the wringing of hands over "draconian colonial laws" brought in and enforced by the British before 1947. But why has the world's largest democracy continued to remain shackled by them? The answers lies not only in their provenance but also in the way identity politics has played out in post-independence India.

Karuna Nundy, Supreme Court litigator and vociferous campaigner for civil liberties, tells Index that it is time to subject all these colonial laws to comprehensive review and overhaul. Without discounting the need to tackle hate speech, for which these laws come in handy, she argues that certain provisions of these laws are ludicrous. "Take Section 298, for instance. Besides any words and gestures, certain sounds are also regarded as having the potential to offend religious sentiments. Now, what type of sounds can have such effect? Dog whistles? Wolf whistles? Not by any stretch of imagination." Criminalising each such minute potentially offensive act, with a paranoid appreciation of lurking dangers, militates against every tenet of democracy, she says.

But why aren't legal challenges being mounted to these laws? Nundy says that in several cases the Supreme Court has left it

ABOVE: LGBT activists in front of the Bangalore City Hall during the Pride parade in 2013

to the legislature to decide or uphold them. Those flying the free speech flag have to proceed with caution, in case a verdict makes matters worse.

Only the most naive optimist would have believed that independence from British rule would immediately be accompanied by India's breaking free from the shackles of colonialism's practices and politics. Moreover, given that independence came in the wake of a bloody partition, it was a foregone conclusion that for the newborn state considerations of preserving communal harmony and territorial integrity and averting anarchy would easily trump those of freedom of expression.

All the same, the first amendment to the Indian constitution was a study in paranoia and authoritarian statism, with some concessions made to classical liberalism. Freedom of speech and expression was made contingent on "reasonable restrictions": the state was empowered to curtail speech on the very same grounds as the British had, with an array of measures allowing censorship. As lawyer Lawrence Liang told the Sarai Reader, Prime Minister Jawaharlal Nehru's imperatives of nation-building and maintaining public order compelled him to brush aside the reservations of his colleagues and grant the state sweeping powers to regulate speech.

Little has changed in the intervening years – except to get worse. Securing and maintaining India's territorial integrity remains a top priority, even if it comes at the cost of denying the people of Kashmir their right to self-determination. More significantly, the offence of sedition (in Section 124 A of the IPC) has been used most brutally and arbitrarily against the people of Kashmir or anyone who speaks on their behalf. Laws against sedition go back to the 16th century in English common law. Sedition legislation, used against fighters for independence in India, was extended in scope with an amendment in 1898, a draconian law that allows

the state to crush the smallest murmurs of dissent.

What has made matters worse is the massive surge in militant Hindu nationalism in the past 40 years. Of course, Hindu nationalism had been part of the anti-colonial movement, but it was only from the 1970s that advocates of Hindutva – the political-religious ideology of militant Hindu supremacy – really started to make their mark on politics and society, with disastrous results for freedom of expression. Hindutva's first goal was to politicise historiography in order to advance its founders' claims that Indian history begins with the ascent of indigenous Aryans, that true Hinduism is moored in the Vedic canons, and to advance arguments that Muslims and Christians cannot legitimately call themselves indigenous.

"A claim to history is now being used to forcefully legitimise an opinion," Romila Thapar, one of India's most distinguished historians, said recently in an interview with The Hindu. She should know, having faced the ire of Hindutva's footsoldiers. In 2003, the US Library of Congress acknowledged her contribution by appointing her to the prestigious Kluge Chair for the Countries and Cultures of the South. Immediately, a vitriolic campaign was unleashed against her. She was accused of being "an avowed antagonist of India's Hindu civilisation... who has indulged in cultural genocide".

The Hindu nationalist parties aren't alone in repressing free expression. In →

→ 1976, the Congress government in Uttar Pradesh banned social historian and cultural activist Periyar's Ramayan: A True Reading ostensibly because the anti-majoritarian, anti-Aryan narrative of the book had hurt Hindus' feelings. Subsequently, the Supreme Court not only quashed the ban, but also took the government to task for pandering to upper-caste Hindu voters.

In 1987, the Congress government in Maharashtra reneged on its undertaking to publish Bhimrao Ramji Ambedkar's Riddles of Hinduism because of the book's strident anti-Brahminical tone, and obviously because it did not want to antagonise the right-wing Shiv Sena and upper-caste Hindus.

The Hoot's Free Speech Tracker blog details dozens of examples of activists and journalists being charged with sedition –

She doesn't foresee any of these colonial legal cobwebs being swept away

including Arvind Kejriwal, the former chief minister of Delhi. "The panopticon of the national security state, which is growing bigger and bigger, poses one of the gravest threats to freedom of expression and completely squashes any attempts of citizens seeking accountability from their government," says. Geeta Seshu, veteran journalist and consulting editor of The Hoot. It has been assiduously tracking freedom of expression in India and the subcontinent. She doesn't foresee any of these colonial legal cobwebs being swept away: they are too useful politically. She points to one instance after another of bruised sentiments and "national interest" being used to stifle freedom of expression.

In the aftermath of the supreme court's decision last year to overrule Justice A P

Shah and criminalise gay sex on the basis of a 153-year-old law (Section 377), there was further discussion of why colonial legislation was still in place. The issue hit the news headlines internationally, and the India Supreme Court has agreed to review its decision, but as Index on Censorship magazine went to press there was no indication of when.

The Indian state achieved independence from British rule, but it did not free itself from the framework that the colonial rulers created to maintain stability, and to divide,the population. Indeed, in the post-independence era, the state has discovered what the anthropologist and commentator William Mazzarella calls "the productive uses of censorship". The body of law can be used in pursuit of power by unscrupulous populist politicans – who also use "national security" to suppress dissent, and consolidate power.

Perhaps it is too idealistic to hope for a complete, clean break from the past. But we can do what we can to prevent the Trojan horse of solicitous concerns from sneaking in competitive intolerance. As Thomas Jefferson said, "the price of liberty is eternal vigilance". X

© Saurav Datta
www.indexoncensorship.org

Saurav Datta teaches media law in Bombay and Pune, India. He tweets @sauravdatta29

Brain unboxed

43(2): 127/130 | DOI: 10.1177/0306422014537184

Physics professor and broadcaster Jim Al-Khalili talks about the freedom to teach science, blasphemy laws and why scientists should spend more time with politicians to Index on Censorship editor **Rachael Jolley**

THE WORLD NEEDS more scientists who can translate complicated concepts for normal people. Luckily Jim Al-Khalili is one. For non-scientists, speaking to Al-Khalili is a pleasurable experience. He manages to take ideas that might be out-of-reach for many of us, and simplify them into easy-to-use language, and, hey presto, they makes sense. That's pretty useful for a professor of public engagement in science, which is just one of his roles at the UK's University of Surrey, the other being professor of physics, and his third role, and the one perhaps best known to the general public, is presenter of BBC Radio 4's The Life Scientific, where he gets the chance to interview many of science's big hitters.

His academic credentials are pretty impressive, from a postdoctoral research fellowship at University College London, then on to Surrey to teach and adding science broadcasting to his CV, picking up a host of prizes and accolades along the way, including honorary fellow of the British Science Association and the Royal Society's Michael Faraday prize for science communication. There's also a shelf full of books to his name. Clearly Al-Khalili is not one of those scientists who are rarely seen outside a lab. In fact he believes strongly that scientists have to spend a lot more time speaking to politicians and helping them understanding science research; and working with them on policy.

He is also pretty keen on scientists spending more time talking to the media.

When it comes to science and restrictions on debate, discussion and development, there are several things on his mind. He worries about blasphemy laws and fear of religious offence being used to preclude debate or even teaching about science, particularly evolution.

"If you don't have the policies and laws in place to protect rationalism and science and freedom to question, it's hard for individuals to say: 'I do have the right to say this.'"

It shouldn't be up to individual scientists to have to defend the right and freedom to teach about scientific research, he believes. "The fact is I don't think it should be down to individuals to have to stand their ground." He says the right to teach should be entrenched in the policy of countries, with a separation of science and religion.

The University of Surrey professor also worries about attitudes to science in parts of the Islamic world. Al-Khalili, who grew up in Iraq, says science can be interpreted by some as a Western construct. "They have to see not just the benefits of science to society, more than that they have to understand that doing science is about having the freedom to ask questions about the world around you without worrying about whether it's going to influence or affect your religious thinking." →

ABOVE: Six scientists and one government official were convicted of manslaughter after failing to predict the strength of an earthquake near L'Aquila, Italy in 2009

→ Al-Khalili remembers growing up in Iraq and as a child talking about evolution much more freely than he believes would be the case today. "Colleagues of mine are finding it tough in a way that maybe they didn't 20 years ago." He hears from teachers saying that their students, particularly those from Muslim countries, won't accept evolution.

The MMR scare would not happen today as far more scientists would join the discussion

There are other worries. In 2012 six scientists and one official were convicted of manslaughter in Italy for not predicting the strength of the devastating earthquake in L'Aquila that left more than 300 people dead. The ramifications of the convictions could lead to scientists refusing to make any predictions of environmental impact, because of fears of legal action. "In that sort of environment you're not gong to say anything, and yet it's vital that scientists continue to engage with politicians." One of Al-Khalili's big beefs is scientists failing to communicate with the public and policymakers.

"The bottom line is, if scientists do retreat because they feel under threat then it will just make matters worse, because they will be seen as lacking in transparency, hiding the truth from the public."

Traditionally scientists have not done enough to reach across the divide between politics and academia. "Scientists can no longer leave all the talking to the politicians, there are not enough that are scientifically trained, scientifically literate people."

"What scientists can do is offer the scientific evidence and say: 'On the basis of this we think you should do this, we think you should have a policy on this'."

"They are acknowledging that politicians make choices based on all sorts of things, not just scientific evidence, shame though that is, because they look at economics, they look at culture, public acceptability, and sometimes there's a tension. But scientists have to be there, they have to provide the evidence, they have to explain to policy makers, the importance of evidence-based policies."

As an academic and as a communicator, he is clearly an enthusiast. "We have to be open, we have to be transparent. We have to say this is the evidence and this is what we can, and what we can't, say because these are the risks."

Fear and loathing might describe the relationship between scientists and the media in years gone by, but Al-Khalili believes this is changing. Scientists used to be suspicious of any of their own who even spoke to the media, and felt they were selling out. But at the heart of that struggle, he believes, the two professions didn't understand what each other was seeking. He thinks that gap is being bridged. Although an earlier comment about the science community's reaction to a television programme suggests it hasn't gone away totally.

Al-Khalili says one of the biggest struggles for scientists today is getting politicians to worry about the long term. "The real challenge is for scientists to engage with governments and get them to take some of these things seriously, rather than just thinking about saving their own skin for the next year or two, to take seriously what might be coming down the line in the next decade."

"I think the big challenges that are facing the world are obviously climate change, water, energy, food supplies. Science can play a huge role in mitigating against the worst effects of those."

So how does he think scientists can influence politics and politicians to put a greater emphasis on thinking and acting to protect the decades to come? The answer, he believes, is not with the politicians but with the public. If the public care (because they or their children will suffer the consequences), then they will put pressure on the

ABOVE: Professor Jim Al-Khalili

politicians to act. "So it's not just the politicians that need convincing but the wider society."

"For most people it's just natural to have a keener interest in the immediate. I want to be able to put my central heating on. I want to be able to drive my car. I don't want to change my lifestyle."

He acknowledges that it is not easy and scientists are often seen as alarmist. Despite the scientific evidence about climate change, Al-Khalili feels there is still a huge struggle ahead to convince the public that climate change is real. "I'm not quite sure why there is still such a large fraction of the population and politicians who are sceptical about what's happening, despite all the evidence."

So where are scientists on the GM debate and why does scientific evidence not nec- →

→ essarily persuade the public? "A lot of the worries are unfounded but that doesn't mean they are not rational, based on what the world sees."

He adds: "We eat GM foods all the time. Anything we import from North America is likely to be a GM food. We've been genetically modifying crops for thousands of years. It's just that we're doing it now with more knowledge."

Al-Khalili doesn't believe the MMR scandal, which left hundreds of thousands of parents scared to have their children vaccinated for measles, mumps and rubella, would happen today, as more scientists would join the discussion. The MMR scare stories related to science research published in the medical journal The Lancet, which led to headlines in newspapers, about the risks of the combined MMR vaccine, but the research was eventually discredited. Back then, he says: "Scientists, those working in the health service, just weren't prepared to engage. It was ridiculous that they weren't going to get involved with the discussion."

Reports from the US and Canada recently showed scientists were worried about public funding cuts and impact on their freedom of expression as well as their ability to continue their research. The argument from the US was that research was being held back as scientists were seeing grants for travel to conferences and to complete research cut back. This was particularly heightened during the recent government shutdown. Al-Khalili has referred previously to worries that Peter Higgs would not get the funding today that set the course towards the discovery of Higgs boson, for which he was jointly awarded the Nobel Prize for Physics in 2013 alongside François Englert. Increasingly, science grants are not based on ideas or researching theories but on outcomes, and with a need for an explanation of direct benefits to society, he argues, and that is something society should worry about. "We might miss out big discoveries simply because we're only focusing on what we think has immediate applications. Some of the greatest scientific discoveries in history came about just because people were curious about the world."

And it is obvious that Al-Khalili is going to put his great passion into making sure that discussions about science and discovery continue to be as open as possible. X

© Rachael Jolley
www.indexoncensorship.org

Rachael Jolley is editor of Index on Censorship

Future imperfect

43(2): 131/136 | DOI: 10.1177/0306422014534794

Should concerns about privacy after the NSA revelations change the way we use the web? **Jason DaPonte** asks the experts about state spying, corporate control and what we can do to protect ourselves

"GOVERNMENT MAY PORTRAY itself as the protector of privacy, but it's the worst enemy of privacy and that's borne out by the NSA revelations," web and privacy guru Jeff Jarvis tells Index.

Jarvis, author of Public Parts: How Sharing in the Digital Age Improves the Way We Work and Live argues that this complacency is dangerous and that a debate on "public-ness" is needed. Jarvis defines privacy "as an ethic of knowing someone else's information (and whether sharing it further could harm someone)" and publicness as "an ethic of sharing your own information (and whether doing so could help someone)".

In his book Public Parts and on his blog, he advocates publicness as an idea, claiming it has a number of personal and societal benefits including improving relationships and collaboration, and building trust.

He says in the United States the government can't open post without a court order, but a different principle has been applied to electronic communications. "If it's good enough for the mail, then why isn't it good enough for email?"

While Jarvis is calling for public discussion on the topic, he's also concerned about the "techno panic" the issue has sparked. "The internet gives us the power to speak, find and act as a [single] public and I don't want to see that power lost in this discus-sion. I don't want to see us lose a generous society based on sharing. The revolutionaries [in recent global conflicts] have been able to find each other and act, and that's the power of tech. I hate to see how deeply we pull into our shells," he says.

The Pew Research Centre predicts that by 2025, the "internet will become like electricity – less visible, yet more deeply embedded in people's lives for good and ill." Devices such as Google Glass (which overlays information from the web on to the real world via a pair of lenses in front of your eyes) and internet-connected body monitoring systems like, Nike+ and Fitbit, are all examples of how we are starting to become surrounded by a new generation of constantly connected objects. Using an activity monitor like Nike+ means you are transmitting your location and the path of a jog from your shoes to the web (via a smartphone). While this may not seem like particularly private data, a sliding scale emerges for some when these devices start transmitting biometric data, or using facial recognition to match data with people you meet in the street.

As apps and actions like this become more mainstream, understanding how privacy can be maintained in this environment requires us to remember that the internet is decen-tralised; it is not like a corporate IT network where one department (or person) can →

ABOVE: US citizens and public advocacy organisations rally against NSA spying on Capitol Hill, Washington DC

switch the entire thing off through a top-down control system.

The internet is a series of interconnected networks, constantly exchanging and copying data between servers on the network and then on to the next. While data may take usual paths, if one path becomes unavailable or fails, the IP (Internet Protocol) system re-routes the data. This de-centralisation is key to the success and ubiquity of the internet – any device can get on to the network and communicate with any other, as long as it follows very basic communication rules.

This means there is no central command on the internet; there is no Big Brother unless we create one. This de-centralisation may also be the key to protecting privacy as the network becomes further enmeshed in our everyday lives. The other key is common sense. When asked what typical users should do to protect themselves on the internet, Jarvis had this advice: "Don't be an idiot, and don't forget that the internet is a lousy place to keep secrets. Always remember that what you put online could get passed around."

As the internet has come under increasing control by corporations, certain services, particularly on the web, have started to store, and therefore control, huge amounts of data about us. Google, Facebook, Amazon and others are the most obvious because of the sheer volume of data they track about their millions of users, but nearly every commercial website tracks some sort of behavioural data about its users. We've allowed corporations to gather this data either because we don't know it's happening (as is often the case with cookies that track and save information about our browsing behaviour) or in exchange for better services – free email accounts (Gmail), personalised recommendations (Amazon) or the ability to connect with friends (Facebook).

"A transaction of mutual value isn't surveillance," Jarvis argues, referencing Google's Priority Inbox (which analyses your emails to determine which are "important" based on who you email and the relevance of the subject) as an example. He expands on this explaining that as we look at what is legal in this space we need to be careful to distinguish between how data is gathered and how it is used. "We have to be very, very careful about restricting the gathering of knowledge, careful of regulating what you're allowed to know. I don't want to be in a regime where we regulate knowledge."

Sinister or not, the internet giants and those that aspire to similar commercial success find themselves under continued and increasing pressure from shareholders, marketers and clients to deliver more and more data about you, their customers. This is the big data that is currently being hailed as

The NSA's greatest win would be to convince people that privacy doesn't exist

something of a Holy Grail of business intelligence. Whether we think of it as surveillance or not, we know – at least on some level – that these services have a lot of our information at their disposal (eg the contents of all of our emails, Facebook posts, etc) and we have opted in by accepting terms of service when we sign up to use the service.

"The NSA's greatest win would be to convince people that privacy doesn't exist," says Danny O'Brien, international director of the US-based digital rights campaigners Electronic Frontier Foundation. "Privacy nihilism is the state of believing that: 'If I'm doing nothing wrong, I have nothing to hide, so it doesn't matter who's watching me'."

This has had an unintended effect of creating what O'Brien describes as "unintentional honeypots" of data that tempt those who want to snoop, be it malicious hackers, other corporations or states. In the

→ past, corporations protected this data from hackers who might try to get credit card numbers (or similar) to carry out theft. However, these "honeypot" operators have realised that while they were always subject to the laws and courts of various countries, they are now also protecting their data from state security agencies. This largely came to light following the alleged hacking of Google's Gmail by China. Edward Snowden's revelations about the United States' NSA and the UK's GCHQ further proved the extent to which states were carrying out not just targeted snooping, but also mass surveillance on their own and foreign citizens.

To address this issue, many of the corporations have turned on data encryption; technology that protects the data as it is in transit across the nodes (or "hops") across the internet so that it can only be read by the

Unintentional 'honeypots' of data tempt those who want to snoop, be it maliacious hackers, other corporations or states

intended recipient (you can tell if this is on when you see the address bar in your internet browser say "https" instead of "http"). While this costs them more, it also costs security agencies more money and time to try to get past it. So by having it in place, the corporations are creating a form of "passive activism".

Jarvis thinks this is one of the tools for protecting users' privacy, and says the task of integrating encryption effectively largely lies with the corporations that are gathering and storing personal information.

"Google thought that once they got [users' data] into their world it was safe. That's why the NSA revelations are shocking. It's getting better now that companies are encrypting as they go," he said. "It's become the job of the corporations to protect their customers."

Encryption can't solve every problem though. Codes are made to be cracked and encrypted content is only one level of data that governments and others can snoop on.

O'Brien says the way to address this is through tools and systems that take advantage of the de-centralised nature of the internet, so we remain in control of our data and don't rely on third party to store or transfer it for us. The volunteer open-source community has started to create these tools.

Protecting yourself online starts with a common-sense approach. "The internet is a lousy place to keep a secret," Jarvis says. "Once someone knows your information (online or not), the responsibility of what to do with it lies on them," says Jarvis. He suggests consumers be more savvy about what they're signing up to share when they accept terms and conditions, which should be presented in simple language. He also advocates setting privacy on specific messages at the point of sharing (for example, the way you can define exactly who you share with in very specific ways on Google+), rather than blanket terms for privacy.

Understanding how you can protect yourself first requires you to understand what you are trying to protect. There are largely three types of data that can be snooped on: the content of a message or document itself (eg a discussion with a counsellor about specific thoughts of suicide), the metadata about the specific communication (eg simply seeing someone visited a suicide prevention website) and, finally, metadata about the communication itself that has nothing to do with the content (eg the location or device you visited from, what you were looking at before and after, who else you've recently contacted).

You can't simply turn privacy on and off – even Incognito mode on Google's Chrome browser tells you that you aren't really fully "private" when you use it. While technologies that use encryption and de-centralisation can help protect the first two types of

Privacy protectors

TOR

This tool uses layers of encryption and routing through a volunteer network to get around censorship and surveillance. Its high status among privacy advocates was enhanced when it was revealed that an NSA presentation had stated that "TOR stinks". TOR can be difficult to install and there are allegations that simply being a TOR user can arouse government suspicion as it is known to be used by criminals.
http://www.torproject.org

OTR

"Off the Record" instant messaging is enabled by this plugin that applies end-to-end encryption to other messaging software. It creates a seamless experience once set up, but requires both users of the conversation to be running the plug-in in order to provide protection. Unfortunately, it doesn't yet work with the major chat clients, unless they are aggregated into yet another third-party piece of software, such as Pidgin or Adium.
https://otr.cypherpunks.ca/

Disconnect

This browser plugin tries to put privacy control into your hands by making it clear when internet tracking companies or third parties are trying to watch your behaviour. Its user-friendly interface makes it easier to control and understand. Right now, it only works on Chrome and Firefox.
http://www.disconnect.me

Silent Circle

This is a solution for encrypting mobile communications – but only works between devices in the "silent circle" – so good for certain types of uses but not yet a mainstream solution, as encryption wouldn't extend to all calls and messages that users make. Out-of-circle calls are currently only available in North America.
https://silentcircle.com

content that can be snooped on (specific content and metadata about the communication), there is little that can be done about the third type of content (the location and behavioural information). This is because networks need to know where you are to connect you with other users and content (even if it's encrypted). This is particularly true for mobile networks; they simply can't deliver a call, SMS or email without knowing where your device is.

A number of tools are on the horizon that should help citizens and consumers protect themselves, but many of them don't feel ready for mainstream use yet and, as Jarvis argues, integrating this technology could be primarily the responsibility of internet corporations.

In protecting yourself, it is important to remember that surveillance existed long before the internet and forms an important part of most nation's security plans. Governments are, after all, tasked with protect-

It it important to remember that surveillance existed long before the internet

ing their citizens and have long carried out spying under certain legal frameworks that protect innocent and average citizens.

O'Brien likens the way electronic surveillance could be controlled to the way we control the military. "We have a military and it fights for us…, which is what surveillance agencies should do. The really important thing we need to do with these organisations is to rein them back so they act like a modern civilised part of our national defence rather than generals gone crazy who could undermine their own society as much as enemies of the state."

The good news is that the public – and the internet itself – appear to be at a junction. We can choose between a future where we can take advantage of our abilities to self-correct, de-centralise power and empower →

→ individuals, or one where states and corporations can shackle us with technology. The first option will take hard work; the second would be the result of complacency.

Awareness of how to protect the information put online is important, but in most cases average citizens should not feel that they need to "lock down" with every technical tool available to protect themselves. First and foremost, users that want protection should consider whether the information they're protecting should be online in the first place and, if they decide to put it online, should ensure they understand how the platform they're sharing it with protects them.

For those who do want to use technical tools, the EFF recommends using ones that don't rely on a single commercial third party, favouring those that take advantage of open, de-centralised systems (since the third parties can end up under surveillance themselves). Some of these are listed (see box), most are still in the "created by geeks for use by geeks" status and could be more user-friendly. X

©Jason DaPonte
www.indexoncensorship.org

Jason DaPonte is the managing director of The Swarm and former editor for BBC Mobile

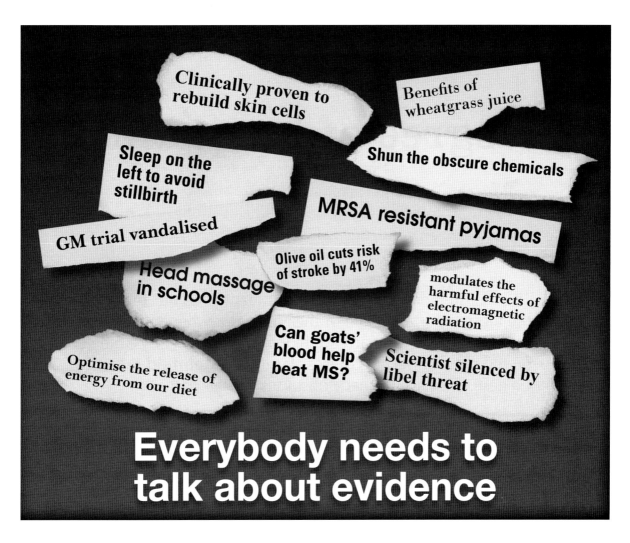

Everybody needs to talk about evidence

Everybody can question claims about risks or benefits – on websites, products, adverts, guidelines, publications or policy announcements – and ask for the evidence.
If more consumers, patients and voters ask for the evidence, those making claims will expect to be held to account.

Ask for evidence is supported by leading scientists, entertainers and community leaders, and many scientific and civic groups. Join the campaign, gets hints and tips on asking for evidence and read stories and advice from other people who have done this at www.senseaboutscience.org/a4e

Sense About Science is a charity that helps people to make sense of science and evidence. We stand up for scientific debate, free from stigma, intimidation, hysteria or censorship. And we encourage everyone, whatever their experience, to insist on evidence in public life.

www.senseaboutscience.org
Registered Charity No. 1146170, Company No. 6771027
🐦 @senseaboutsci   #askforevidence

Degree of inequality

43(2): 138/142 | DOI: 10.1177/0306422014535529

This month thousands of Chinese students find out the results of the most important exam of their lives. But when those results come through, girls have to achieve higher scores than boys to be accepted on the same university courses. **Jemimah Steinfeld** reports on why Chinese girls have so many obstacles in their paths

WHEN XIONG JING read news of four women in the southern city of Guangzhou, China, shaving off their hair to protest against measures making it harder for girls to win places at Chinese universities than boys, she and her co-workers followed suit.

"The first four girls who did it had TV stations filming them. We're in Beijing and it's risky to shave our heads in public. So we did it in our office and posted pictures to Weibo," Xiong tells Index. Xiong works at Gender Watch, a Chinese NGO tackling the issue of gender discrimination. The company's page on Weibo, the Chinese equivalent of Twitter, is the most prominent platform in the country fighting for women's rights. Prior to shaving their heads, Xiong and her co-workers tried to find out from the Chinese ministry of education why there were unfair quotas. The response was unsatisfactory. The government said that it was based on "national interest" but did not elaborate on what that meant.

"We were furious about this," she says. After uploading the photos of herself and her co-workers, 20 others shaved their heads in solidarity, all posting their pictures online. Thousands more expressed their support.

Two years on from the event, Xiong's hair has grown back. Gender discrimination, on the other hand, remains in place in the university sector. As Chinese students sit the national college entrance exam this June, known in China as the *gaokao*, there's still work to be done on gender equality.

University admission in China is based solely on the *gaokao*. Approximately nine million students take it over three days each June and find out in the summer whether they've been admitted to the university and degree course of their choice. No additional material is expected of applicants, making the process transparent in theory. The reality is different.

Reports first started to circulate in 2005 of restrictive practices against women, according to Chinese news outlets. Girls were being banned from studying a variety of subjects across the country, from engineering to navigation. At the same time, they were expected to score higher than boys to get into the same universities for the same courses.

Different reasons were given. For example, police or military-affiliated academies claimed their courses were too dangerous for women. Women not being able to carry heavy equipment and not being able to

ABOVE: A weeping graduate is comforted during her graduation ceremony at Fudan University in Shanghai last June. Women often have to achieve higher entry-level grades than their male counterparts to reach university and are blocked from some courses

escape a mine as quickly as men in an emergency were reasons cited for lower admissions on mining courses.

In another example, Beijing's People's Police University told the BBC that it limits the number of girls admitted to 10-15 per cent of the student body because, apparently, there are fewer jobs open to them after graduation, since most people in China expect police officers to be male.

Meanwhile, certain language courses, such as Arabic and Russian, have raised the bar for women with the argument that the coun-

tries where these languages are spoken are not receptive to women, so there would be

Dong Qi is a headhunter in Beijing. She is often asked by companies for only male applicants

a reduced likelihood of jobs at the end of the degree for these graduates.

ABOVE: Over 6,000 job-seeking graduates line up at a job fair at Tianjin University in the north east of the country

→ The argument that certain degrees and, in turn, jobs can be done only by men is largely unchallenged in Chinese society. Index spoke to secondary school student Yin Meimei, who attends a prestigious boarding school in Chengdu, Sichuan province. She has studied hard for the *gaokao* and hopes to score a top mark, which will enable her to major in Korean at university. But she is aware that in order to obtain a place at a top college in China, she needs to score higher than her male peers, and therefore she's looking at the option of studying in South Korea instead. Yin is also good at science and yet she has never considered subjects like engineering.

"I'm a girl. I cannot do these subjects. They are dangerous and require strong men," says Yin when Index asks her about it.

These arguments conceal the real reason behind the unfair quotas. Chinese girls are consistently scoring better than boys in the admissions tests, leading to a higher percentage being admitted compared to men. Universities are, therefore, instituting a form of affirmative action in favour of less qualified boys. In short, women have become victims of their own success.

Chinese women have done extremely well in terms of education over the past decade. The ratio of female admissions stood at 51.9 per cent in 2013, rising from 43.8 per cent in 2004, according to figures from the ministry of education. However, China is still unprepared for women to have an equal footing to men.

Are you planning a family?

Women are regularly asked for personal information about their lives when job hunting, writes Hannah Leung

Wei Jia, 30, has been working in human resources since she graduated from college in Beijing.

"Employers usually ask female candidates about their love life and family situations. Some press for intimate details about their marriage and pregnancy plans," she tells Index.

While Wei herself has faced these difficult questions during her job search two years ago – she has been married for six years with no children – she has asked them herself when interviewing other women. These private matters are often of concern for companies in assessing how big a liability a female employee is, as companies are required to pay women maternity allowance and give maternity leave. Article 13 of China's labour law states that women and men hold equal employment rights and that the bar for employment standards should not be raised for women.

"Jobs that require you to travel often or entertain clients would of course prefer men, or single women with no family obligations," says Wei. Men, however, never face the same scrutiny over marital or familial obligations.

At 29, Feng Junying will soon be graduating from Beijing Jiatong University's MBA programme. She thinks of these questions as routine, and finds it humorous how far into her personal future human resources personnel have ventured. "During my last interview at a bank, they asked me where my boyfriend lived, what province he was from, and if we had plans to move in together," Feng says. "I don't define myself or what I can do with my career by whether or not I have a boyfriend."

Complicating the matter is the change to China's one-child policy made late last year. The change allows couples to have a second child if one partner is a single child. Though this may seem a progressive shift in policy, a possible side-effect is further pressure for women during job interviews. The state-owned news agency Xinhua ran a story in March 2014 about a mother of a 10-month-old daughter experiencing difficulty finding a job. Employees were reluctant to hire her after discovering that she was a single child. The company feared she would have another child under the new policy, as it's a common assumption that women will try for a son if they first have a daughter.

"The two-child policy may cultivate even more sexism in the work environment," according to the Xinhua article – adding that such discrimination, while rampant, is also almost impossible to prove, as companies will cite other reasons for why a woman is not hired.

Feng is now currently interviewing for jobs. She finds questions about a woman's family plans unproductive but also inevitable.

In the meantime, there are plenty of discussion boards online guiding women on how to navigate the issue. Users on Chinese online forum Zihu.com address a woman's enquiry: "What's the best way to answer the typical questions women face during job interviews, concerning marriage and children?" The general consensus seems to be that women need to keep talking about the issue.

©Hannah Leung
www.indexoncensorship.org

Credit: (right) iStock/Getty/yuyanga

ABOVE: Chinese mothers with just one daughter could be discriminated against by employers

Hannah Leung is a freelance journalist, based in Beijing

Discrimination against women in China starts before they're even born. Within the context of the one-child policy, a combination of sex-selective abortion and female infanticide has led to a ratio of 100 girls to every 118 boys. Gender bias continues throughout their lives. As the university quotas highlight, it's a question of employment too. In China's workforce it is normal for women to be banned from certain jobs because of a perception that they are only suited to men.

Dong Qi is a headhunter in Beijing. In an interview with Index, Dong says she is often asked by companies for only male applicants. These jobs are usually in the fields of engineering or involve foreign travel. But even industries more commonly associated

Images circulate of women wearing university graduation gowns who are unable to wed

with women impose gender restrictions. In January, news circulated of a young woman in Beijing, Cao Ju, taking a private tutor company, Juren Academy, to court after it refused to employ her for a teaching job because she was female. The case was the first of its kind. While these practices go on constantly, they're very hard to fight.

This is part of a bigger problem. The Chinese government closely controls the number of outlets through which people can voice their grievances. Gender Watch is one of only a few NGOs devoted to raising awareness about gender inequality. And they've got their work cut out. Xiong says that after they shaved their heads, they approached several lawyers to seek advice. The lawyers said they would offer legal aid to any clients wanting to fight barriers against women. But finding victims to represent has been difficult. One girl reached out to Xiong on Weibo. She did not get into her first-choice university →

→ and discovered she had higher grades than men who did. She got into her second choice though and in the end decided against pursuing the lawsuit out of fear that the government would rescind her university offer.

"The government has a tight grip on civil society. These gender biases have permeated society from pre-birth. They require a top-down initiative, but so far the government is doing the exact opposite. When you boil it down it's really a one-party problem," says author and academic Leta Hong Fincher. Her recent book, Leftover Women: The Resurgence of Gender Inequality in China, explores the topic of pressure on women to leave the workforce, get married and fulfill more traditional roles.

In 2013 the education ministry issued a new regulation saying that only a few universities could legitimately discriminate against women

"I see a concerted backlash against the tremendous educational gains for women," Hong Fincher tells Index.

"There's no indication that the Chinese government is concerned about a drop in female labour participation. On the contrary, you see in the rhetoric of 'leftover women' messages to go back to the home."

Hong Fincher's book outlines the effects of a government-sponsored effort to guilt-trip women into marrying early. Chinese women are labelled leftover if single and over the age of 27. Images circulate of women wearing university graduation gowns who are unable to wed. These educated women are the subject of ridicule. The images are internalised by women. They affect their ambitions and deter them from being more vocal when confronted by discrimination.

In the two years since the women shaved their heads and the issue gained real traction, there has been some progress. In 2013 the education ministry issued a new regulation saying that only a few universities could legitimately discriminate against women. Then, during the annual National People's Congress meetings in March this year, some representatives raised the issue again. These actions will be of comfort to some, but not to all. China has plenty of policies in place that enshrine principles of equality. The country is founded on the Maoist principle that women hold up half the sky alone. What's lacking is a government commitment to enforce these principles and, as these examples highlight, when it comes to China progress is not always linear. X

©Jemimah Steinfeld
www.indexoncensorship.org

Jemimah Steinfeld worked as a reporter in Beijing for CNN, Huffington Post and Time Out. Her new book Little Emperors and Material Girls: Sex and Youth in Modern China is out at the end of the year

Do small media now control the news agenda?

OPINION

43(2): 143/147 | DOI: 10.1177/0306422014535687

Bruno Torturra, founder of Brazilian citizen journalism project Mídia Ninja, says traditional media companies have been left behind by innovation and no longer hold all the power. **Richard Sambrook**, journalism professor and former BBC World Service director, disagrees

Bruno Torturra

The "big media" face a crisis of economics and a crisis of credibility. Small media are certainly driving the modern news agenda. Firstly, because they are a way to connect and map public interest. And also because the so-called big media are having difficulties spreading their coverage across all the issues that now matter to people.

We started Mídia Ninja [the Ninja comes from Narrativas Independentes, Jornalismo e Ação and translates as "Independent Narrative Journalism and Action"] in 2011, because we wanted to create web shows and TV in cities and regions across Brazil that barely have local media. It was also to open a new frontier in free debate and speech, which are being constrained by the consolidation of mainstream media. It's not traditional censorship, but big media do present a monolithic narrative worldwide, which alienates lots of people. The cable news in the USA is a good example. MSBC, Fox and even CNN are much more defined by their narratives than their news or scoops. Their public follows them not necessarily because of their trustworthiness, but because of their narratives.

Richard Sambrook

Richard Sambrook

Most people in the world today still find out their news from big media. The →

Bruno Torturra

→ internet and social media have revitalised news, information and how we learn about the world – and will continue to do so. However, that does not mean we should abandon, ignore or tear up the best of the past. There is much wrong with big media, but also much that is right and good, which has been learned in the crucible of pressurised news coverage of major events over many decades. That should be recognised and built upon.

Big newspapers and broadcasters are still at the heart of the major issues – for the obvious reasons that they have the reach or circulation to ensure a story is read, seen or heard by the most people. As a consequence, big media have influence – with politicians, with business, with opinion formers, as well as with their audience or readers. They also

There is much wrong with big media but there is also much that is right and good

have the resources and institutional weight to take on vested interests and withstand pressure – for example, The Guardian with the Snowden revelations.

Large news organisations can afford to employ full-time media lawyers, they can engage barristers to fight their corner in court, they have the budgets to resist being sued and they have the institutional weight that will make some think twice before embarking on malicious legal action. Small companies often have none of this and, as such, are more vulnerable to legal pressures and to making less informed decisions when under political attack.

Bruno Torturra

I believe big media have failed in many ways. The democratisation of public dialogue should have provoked a huge change in economics, ethics and language. The

media should have become more plural and accountable. To be brief: they failed us by fighting a wave they could have surfed.

I believe this has to do with two things: changing metrics (instead of just clicks, circulation and numbers, focus on engagement and quality of the buzz); and changing income streams (instead of adverts, invest in events, education and public debates, and engage in changing public policy). It's also important to understand something basic: digitalisation of information is not just a technological advance. It demands a change in mentality and a change in the meaning of journalism.

We were planning to build our company much more slowly. Then the huge protests came along in Brazil. The official narrative was the usual one: that protesters were vandals who started the violence. Way more airtime was given to rubbish bins being burned than unarmed people being beaten by the police. There were no discussions at all about the constitutional rights of protesters. Apart from some brave photographers, there were barely any reporters on the ground.

Because of our agility, our national presence and the way we challenge the official and predictable media narrative, we were catapulted to fame in days. Hundreds of people joined, we were able to cover more than 100 cities and produce tons of information. But it was a process that was impossible to manage. So, instead of trying to control it, we opened the network and gave absolute freedom to our collaborators and reporters. Mídia Ninja triggered a national debate about the role and definition of journalism.

We were able, countless times, to change the public conversation about the country's protests, police violence, the public workers' strikes. We didn't rely on big broadcasters picking up the story. Every single time we made the "big news" it was because it already was a huge story, already spreading out on the web. Of course, it had to do with the quality and relevance of our material, but also because of the public disappointment with the big media, and the hunger for a new way of producing and narrating news.

Richard Sambrook

What citizen journalism is good at is providing evidence from the ground that mainstream organisations have been unable to get, and providing an outlet for a greater range of voices. But citizen journalism is no more or less "the truth" than any other kind of journalism. It may have an authenticity because it appears to be broadcast or published directly without the filters of editors and organisations in between. However, the term is increasingly confusing and unhelpful, I think. What many call citizen journalism is activism, lobbying or professional journalism delivered by different means and with a different flavour.

I believe good journalism – at any level – should apply a discipline of verification, evidence, analysis and explanation to provide high-quality information to the public. In theory, anyone can do that. In practice, it takes skill and experience.

There are incredibly brave individuals in Syria using their mobile phones to tell the world about the conflict there. But, at the other end of the scale, there are hoaxers, trying to con the public into believing something that isn't true. And there's every shade in between. That's why it's increasingly important for the public to be media literate, to be able to assess and understand what they are seeing. One role for professional media is to do that for the public. Trusted brands among big media can verify, aggregate and curate information – including citizen journalism – so the public understand what they are consuming.

Bruno Torturra

People ask if we can trust citizen journalism, but I could also ask: how can we trust conventional journalism? I believe the same process that empowered citizens as reporters, will soon empower them to be fact-checkers, pundits, ombudsmen. A multiple, more diverse media environment tends to be more trustworthy as a whole. The same premise is behind the very idea of democracy. Can we trust citizen journalists? The best answer I can give you is "as much as you can trust the citizen".

If we make a mistake, we correct it. Often we're called out by the public: fact-checking is a public activity now. We've apologised not only about errors, but also when we regret an opinion or position, expressed by us or a collaborator. This is crucial to us.

Some distortion is, unfortunately, intrinsic to human communication. I believe that

Citizen journalism is no more or less the truth than any other kind of journalism

citizen networks can be more accountable and self-correct more quickly by their very nature. Reputation is of the essence.

Given the horrible quality of online comments in general – here in Brazil, the comments box is often a playground for haters, trolls and racists – I can understand how some big newspapers don't open to comments, but it's almost futile. People will comment and share it anyway on social media.

If we didn't have citizen journalists, the world would be less democratic, less informed, less interesting and with a much more entrenched political elite.

Richard Sambrook

The public do need to trust the media. Accountability is a clear part of that. What happens if the public have a complaint that isn't recognised as legitimate by a Mídia Ninja? Is there any form of arbitration or process where they can get their concerns →

→ addressed? Simply saying "We will apologise if we make a mistake" is good as far as it goes, but news coverage is more complicated than that. Sometimes organisations don't recognise they have made mistakes and the public feel powerless to get a legitimate concern recognised.

Do big media companies bring higher standards and tougher regulations? It's not black or white. Broadcasters in the UK are regulated to be impartial and to follow a code of conduct. Newspapers aren't. Yet there are some newspapers that have very high editorial standards and there are occasions when broadcasters don't. The debate over press regulation in the UK following the Leveson inquiry has been about how to make the press accountable without infring-

Small media are still learning to be more autonomous and dig out stories on their own

ing its independence. That conundrum hasn't yet been solved.

However, most big news organisations have a code of conduct and a complaints procedure. Corporate media have shareholders to whom they are accountable. Small media often don't have any form of public accountability.

Bruno Torturra

Editing is our biggest challenge. During the riots, it was a chaotic process. As we never had a proper office or official positions, the editing was being done on the go – on mobile phones – or sometimes not at all.

It's also important to recognise that small media are still driven by the big media. Small media are still learning to be more autonomous and capable of digging out stories on their own. We're getting there.

Would the big media of today collapse without small companies feeding into them?

My short answer would be yes. But the biggest menace to them is their own commercial and centralised mentality – the idea that information is, first and foremost, a business, and an essentially competitive one. It's not, and it shouldn't be. Certainly media enterprises have to generate money, that goes without saying, but the resources have to come from an economy based on collaboration, not mere competition.

We can come up with more diverse and creative ways of financing media. We live in the age in which the public are no longer passive. The ideal, in my opinion, is for new media companies to be financed directly by the public: from donations, parties, courses, lectures, taxpayers' money (in some cases), foundations, the products we produce. Smaller and more agile outlets don't need much money.

I hope that small companies, collectives and more agile media players will help to update the big media. It would be sad and dangerous to see big newspapers, TV channels and media groups go bankrupt. But it's up to them to get their acts together.

Richard Sambrook

There is often an assumption that the tenets of social media will increasingly be necessary for success (collaboration, open working, networked coverage). However, many of the most successful media companies work in almost the opposite way – they are closed, dictatorial, highly directional. And they produce material the public enjoy and pay for in significant numbers. The MailOnline (the UK Daily Mail's website) with its celebrity coverage is an obvious example: highly profitable, globally popular, but there is nothing collaborative, or open about it. In the end, the public decide what they want to consume – and it will include some small media examples, some open and collaborative models, but it will also continue to include big media acting like big media for the foreseeable future.

I'm not sure I'd agree that big media would collapse without the smaller players, but it would certainly be a lot less interesting. They might well stagnate, which is not quite the same thing. Small media can innovate, can take creative risks, in ways big media can't or find it very difficult to do. That innovation is vital in media, including in news. And the innovation that starts somewhere small can swiftly grow to become mainstream. Look at how data journalism has come through to be an important part of our information diet.

Big and small media can be complementary. Take Channel 4, one of the UK's major broadcasters: it was established explicitly to commission production from the independent sector, which has led to a diversity of voices and the nurturing of production and on-screen talent that might have struggled to succeed elsewhere. Also look at the freelance journalists who have found their work in major news outlets. It doesn't always work harmoniously – but corporate and independent media can support and complement each other to the benefit of all.

Ultimately, as an avid news consumer, I benefit by being able to have all forms of media, from all over the world, available to me at my fingertips. ☒

© Bruno Torturra, Richard Sambrook
www.indexoncensorship.org

Richard Sambrook is the director of the Centre for Journalism at Cardiff School of Journalism, Media and Cultural Studies, and former director of the BBC World Service

Bruno Torturra is a journalist and founder of Brazilian citizen journalism network Mídia Ninja

Changing the channel

43(2): 148/151 | DOI: 10.1177/0306422014535690

Argentina's president, Cristina Fernández de Kirchner, has used emergency TV broadcasts nine times in the first four months of 2014, and for reasons that are often relatively trivial. **Adrian Bono** reports from Buenos Aires on the leader's love of one-way communication

A **WAVING ARGENTINIAN** flag unexpectedly invades the screen as television stations interrupt their regular programming to make way for the sight and sounds of an ecstatic crowd. Thousands of people jump up and down, raise banners carrying party slogans, chant about revolutions, and repeat Peronist mantras over and over.

A female presenter announces that President Cristina Fernández de Kirchner is about to address "the 40 million Argentinians" from a meeting celebrating the spoken word, at the Tecnópolis science and technology park in Buenos Aires. The crowd goes wild, as if they were attending a rock concert rather than a regular political rally. As the build-up reaches a crescendo, Fernández grabs the microphone and tells the crowd to "listen up", before introducing a rapper and a stand-up comedian, who perform on stage as the entire country listens.

This, for the audience at home, is where things take a surreal twist. Having programming interrupted for the *cadena nacional* (national broadcast) is not unusual in itself – especially under Fernández's presidency, during which time televised speeches have become increasing common. But for a burst of light entertainment? Fernandez insisted the occasion – the opening of a new exhibit "that celebrates the use of the word" – was

important. News channels, who live-tweeted the announcements as usual, ended up sounding bizarre in their dead-pan delivery: "#NOW on the National Broadcast, the rapper Mustafá Yoda".

The national broadcast – in Argentina, as well as in other Latin American countries – enables the head of state to simultaneously interrupt the normal programming of network television and radio stations in order to address the population. Traditionally, it has been used to convey an important message, or to address the population on holidays, such as Independence Day or the anniversary of the Falklands War.

With less than two years left in office and her popularity waning, Fernández seems to be increasing reliant on the national broadcast to reassure the public and speak out against her critics. By early April this year, she had already used it nine times. Sometimes to unveil a new policy; sometimes to talk down her critics; sometimes just to show she is still at the helm. In January, she was unusually silent for almost six weeks, sparking fears about her health, following brain surgery last October. She returned with a typically defiant broadcast: "I hope nobody criticises this nationally televised address after demanding my presence so much."

ABOVE: Cristina Fernández de Kirchner delivers a speech at the Casa Rosada, the presidential palace in Buenos Aires

Argentina has been under the rule of the Victory Front party for 11 years now. Néstor Kirchner served as president from 2003 to 2007, and was followed in the role by his wife, who was elected after her husband's first term, re-elected in 2011, and is expected to leave office by the end of next year as she is constitutionally prevented from running for a third term.

But ever since a conflict over export duties with the farming sector in 2008 created a division in public opinion, the presidential couple has had a polarising effect on the population. Although Kirchner's sudden death from a heart attack in 2010 caused a temporary surge in sympathy for his widow, opinion continues to be divided.

Fernández is heavily criticised for her decision to bypass the media on a regular basis and resort to one-way channels of communication, such as social media and the national broadcast. Historically, the broadcast has always been considered an effective medium for reaching the population, especially in times of dire need, such as in December 2001, when then president Fernando De la Rúa used it to declare martial law amid growing social unrest that would end with his resignation only a few hours later. →

→ The Broadcast Media Law, which was passed by Congress in 2009, regulated the national broadcast, stating that "in exceptional or grave situations, as well as in those of institutional relevance", the executive branch could make use of the airwaves to send a message across the entire country. But even though it was Fernández who spearheaded the media law, she has been accused of predominantly using the national broadcast as a tool for political propaganda. Many consider most of her announcements as neither exceptional, nor grave, nor relevant.

Ever since she was elected, Fernández has barely spoken to reporters. Her obligation, she says, "is to inform the public about her acts of government", not respond to journalists' questions. Whenever she is accused of not speaking to the press, she replies that

Ever since she was elected, Fernández has barely spoken to reporters

"she speaks every day", and that is mostly true, except that she's referring to the extensive media coverage of her political rallies and ceremonies that, until recently, used to happen on an almost daily basis. With the exception of television channel Todo Noticias, currently at odds with her administration after the Broadcast Media Law forced its parent company Grupo Clarín to divest, all other news networks regularly broadcast her speeches live.

Surrounded by hundreds of supporters and cabinet members who cheer and applaud, Fernández's addresses tend to follow a simple modus operandi: first, she announces the reason for making use of the national broadcast – which could be the inauguration of a new school or a rise in pensions. After the presentation, her speech becomes more political, confrontational, and usually focuses on criticising – directly or

indirectly – the media or the opposition, as she constantly reminds the population of her administration greatest achievements. During her time in office, the national broadcast has been used to blast the judiciary after an unfavorable ruling, to announce the creation of a new credit line for small and medium-sized businesses, and to inform the country about her decision to convert all her savings in dollars to pesos, in a display of patriotism that she hoped would set an example that many others would follow. Her messages can range from 20 minutes to four hours, and their use seems to have increased since her party suffered a terrible defeat in the midterm elections last October.

Critics have compared Fernández to other regional leaders, such as Ecuador's Rafael Correa and the late president of Venezuela Hugo Chávez, both known for their crusades against large media groups, and for making an extensive use of their own national broadcasts – with Chávez once speaking before the cameras for over nine hours.

When Fernández does, very occasionally, agree to a press interview, it has often led to criticism. The chosen reporter is usually ideologically aligned with her government and focuses on anecdotal chat, instead of pitching hardball questions about inflation, poverty or corruption. Meanwhile, major political leaders in the opposition, such as Buenos Aires mayor Mauricio Macri or lawmaker Sergio Massa, have embraced the press conference, engaged in debates and appeared as guests on television shows.

During overseas trips, Fernández has sometimes been confronted with the inevitable press conference, but she is quick to cast aside any unwanted questions about domestic policy with a simple answer: this is neither the time nor the place to discuss that. Most notably, in September 2012, she was invited to give speeches in the universities of Harvard and Georgetown, in the United States. On both occasions, she was greeted with packed auditoriums, with not only college students but also Argentinian expats. In Argentina, the speeches were broadcast live – albeit not via national broadcast – by most media outlets.

She spoke about her administration's many accomplishments – especially those resonating better with the international community, such as marriage equality and the persecution of human rights violators. But it was the unavoidable question and answer session that turned the experience sour, since attendees took the opportunity to ask the kind of questions that journalists in Argentina never could. Begrudgingly, she was forced to provide students with answers, from her rapidly increasing wealth during her time in office to accusations of cooking the books to conceal inflation. She came over as arrogant, defensive and outside of her comfort zones. The Argentinian media had a field day, and she immediately took to Twitter to perform damage control.

Just like the national broadcast, social networks, such as Facebook, YouTube and Twitter, have also been an extremely effective tool for Fernández. With over 2.6 million followers on Twitter, she manages to impact audiences and keep them engaged by sending a stream of tweets – sometimes more than 50 at a time. By applying her colloquial style and often adding jokes, she has a knack for firing up her followers, outraging her detractors, and provoking extensive media coverage.

One such occasion was when, in 2013, several European countries refused to let Bolivian president Evo Morales's plane enter their airspace over suspicions that NSA whistleblower Edward Snowden was onboard. Fernández's post-midnight account of the phone conversations she held with regional leaders as they tried to handle the crisis was followed by millions of outraged Twitter users in South America, and the rest of the world. There was no need to talk to the press directly. Most media outlets in the region immediately picked up her tweets – which sounded dramatic, frantic and ripped from a spy novel – without her having to speak to a single reporter.

Her tweeting may make her seem more accessible, but, aside from very few occasions when she decided to address some praise or criticism that someone posted on her Facebook account, Fernández does not reply to what her constituents say to her online. Many reporters feel they have no choice but to reprint her tweets, and write articles that read like an official press release.

The media in Argentina is far from perfect. Big media groups, including Clarín and La Nación, regularly run headlines critical of the president on the front pages of their newspapers, many of them misleading, anecdotal or purely hyperbolic. This, in turn, has validated the president's accusations against what she calls "the opposition press". Now, whenever a media outlet presents a legitimate claim against the administration, many are prompted to question its veracity. And in turn, it serves as the perfect reason for the president to bypass the media to keep the message from being distorted.

As the use of the national broadcast increases and its content becomes more diverse, many not only consider its use unjustified but also a mockery of itself. Each time one is announced, people turn to their social network of choice to support her, criticise her, make fun of her and wonder what her next announcement will be about.

In the end, if Fernández is looking for people to pay attention to her message and discuss it around the water cooler, while it may not help her garner any additional supporters, her strategy is working.

The population is listening. ☒

© Adrian Bono
www.indexoncensorship.org

Adrian Bono is a journalist at Infobae and founder of The Bubble, an English-language news site in Argentina (bubblear.com)

Real-time news slips out of North Korea

43(2): 152/155 | DOI: 10.1177/0306422014536496

Although all North Korea's media remains state-controlled, there is a growing number of exiles, defectors and brave residents who are striving to get information out. Looking beyond censorship and sensationalism, **Sybil Jones** shares first-hand knowledge of the world behind its border

AFTER JUST A few days in Pyongyang on a tour, I got a fleeting glimpse of what "mind numbing" really means. The TV news in the hotel's restaurant showed the country's dictator Kim Jong Un being applauded by army officers, intercut with similar footage of his late father Kim Jong Il and grandfather Kim Il Sung, while a gushing voice imparted their glories over triumphant brass music. It was the same the day before, and the days before that, and in the previous weeks and during visits made years before. It doesn't change. North Korean "news" serves to glorify the Kims and further the cause of the revolution. Objective indigenous journalism, officially, doesn't exist (hence North Korea is placed 179th out of 180 countries listed on Reporters Sans Frontieres' World Press Freedom Index 2014). In a land with so little reference to the outside world – even the country's calendar counts the years since the birth of the late Great Leader Kim Il Sung – days can pass in a blur.

In March, 100 per cent of voters used their ballots to kiss the Respected Marshal by proxy and endorse Kim Jong Un's rule as always- for every Kim has scored 100 per cent. Unfortunately, this show of faith couldn't dissuade the United Nations from publishing a report showing how the North Korean government had been committing crimes against humanity against its own people for decades. This time the UN Security Council was urged to bring North Korea's leaders to justice at the International Criminal Court, and more sanctions were applied.

How the North's leaders would be brought to book wasn't really explained – and nor was the difference new sanctions would make when the regime had already survived decades of sanctions that had played a role in killing a tenth of the population by famine.

Unfortunately, too often the world's "free" press reverts to sensationalism in covering North Korea, reporting that Kim Jong Un has demanded that all men have their hair cut like his, or that his uncle was executed by being eaten alive by dogs. Yet there is an ever-growing corps of agencies and think-tanks providing real insights and analysis on North Korea, and as close to real-time news from inside the country as is possible. Since 2012 the Associated Press has had an office

ABOVE: North Korean leader Kim Jong Un poses for a picture with senior military staff in Pyongyang earlier this year

in Pyongyang. While outside North Korea there is a score of agencies, think-tanks and analytical groups fielding insights not just from academics, diplomats and Pyongyangologists but also from an ever-growing and vocal global network of North Korean defectors and exiles, and some incredibly brave souls in-country who insist on getting information out – among them NK News, the Daily NK, North Korea Economy Watch and North Korea Leadership Watch. For all that, there are still Western reporters who, when allowed into North Korea on short chaperoned trips, become infantilised and come out all gleeful with little more than footage of Kim Jong Un's dandruff. Others sneak in as tourists to do "undercover exposés" from guided tours that everyone knows

There are some incredibly brave souls in-country who insist on getting information out

are Potemkin exercises, but are nevertheless so frayed that guides have to ask tourists not to photograph the poverty in plain view.

Tourists can now bring in zoom lenses and video cameras, even mobile phones →

→ that they can use if they sign up with the indigenous Koryo mobile network, albeit digitally segregated from the millions of local subscribers. (There are millions nonetheless.) There's more economic activity than you might think. While the capital was recently so dark and quiet at night you could track single cars crossing town, now the lights are on all night on ever more new buildings, and there are traffic jams. The list of cities foreigners can visit is increasing. You see people looking better dressed and better fed than a decade ago, but mostly you only see, rather than speak to, them. They smile and wave more than they did but they still keep their distance from foreigners. Most of the country remains off-limits for foreigners, but in

After Jang's arrest was broadcast, all state news reels and articles were cleansed of his presence

the bits you are allowed to see, every square inch of soil is planted with crops. Agriculture remains terrifyingly precarious, with grain shortfalls of hundreds of thousands of tons a year. The official guides talk openly about it, though they would never suggest that precious state funds spent on ski resorts and weaponry could go on food instead.

When the Dear Leader Kim Jong Il died in 2011, there were hopes that Kim Jong Un would blow the winds of change into the Stalinist autarchy, bringing the fresh air of democracy and liberal economics from his schooling in Switzerland to the mountains of North Korea. Instead he seemed to have learned how isolated militarised elites can survive on the furtive alchemy of making money out of thin air. He rapidly fired some missiles, test-blasted a nuclear bomb and reasserted the economic priority of meeting the military's needs, embedded by his grandfather in the 1960s.

When I visited Pyongyang's museum of the Korean War, lavishly renovated in 2012, we were greeted by a statue of Kim Il Sung, depicted in his youthful prime. His resemblance to his grandson Kim Jong Un is startling, and we wondered if the resemblance is being played up, as if to bridge time back to the glory days of his grandfather, who is 20 years dead but is still the Eternal President. In his half-century in power, Kim Il Sung led his half of a divided country from under Japanese colonial rule, through the Korean War, to become a rapidly industrialising power and, fleetingly, one of east Asia's richest countries. The period from the 1960s to the early 1980s were the best years, and postcards from that era depict brightly coloured city views and lush hotel interiors. You can see the same views today, only they're now heavily stained with the rust and dust that gathered under Kim Jong Il, whose shorter reign left the country's hillsides cirrhotic with the mass graves of famine.

The state narrative may want to frame the very young Kim Jong Un against the bounteous days of the young Kim Il Sung. Kim Jong Un's self-assertion has involved purging his father's backers in the military and civilian government, including the violent expunging of his uncle-by-marriage, Jang Song Thaek, in body and in print (although not by dogs). After news of Jang's arrest was broadcast last December, all state news articles and news reels (and in North Korea all media is state-owned and directed) were "cleansed" of his presence. Soon after, outside observers monitoring the Korea Central News Agency (www.kcna.kp) and other associated outlets saw tens of thousands of articles, all from before October 2013, simply deleted. It was a classic act of old-school Soviet censorship, but with the technology of the web making it instant and globally visible.

Many people believe change will be prompted by China. But Beijing doesn't want its buffer ally of 60 years to collapse – not with the huge US military presence in

South Korea. Meanwhile, the joint US-South Korean war games went ahead this year as they do every year, and as ever they irritate the North. Each side cites the other's military excesses to justify its own massive arms piles. The six-party talks aimed at ending the North's nuclear program start and stall, diplomatic breakthroughs are followed by missile tests, and it's predicted that later in 2014 Pyongyang will do another nuclear bomb test.

But none of that will register in Pyongyang, where the massive images of the Kims beam down from all around, reassuring everyone that all is as it should be and shall remain. The revolution continues – and everything keeps coming back to how it was. ☒

www.indexoncensorship.org

Sybil Jones is a pseudonym for a journalist who reports regularly from North Korea

ABOVE: Celebrating the 20th anniversary of South Africa's first democratic elections, Pretoria, 27 April 2014

CULTURE

In this section

Stage directions in South Africa

43(2): 158/163 | DOI: 10.1177/0306422014534578

On the 20th anniversary of South African democracy actor/director
Dame Janet Suzman looks back and forward at protest in plays

THE MARKET THEATRE sits in downtown Johannesburg, just south of the railway station that bisects the city. It was designated a "grey area" – neither white nor black. Apartheid's blanket laws did not specify usage in the grey areas, and thus the location was perfect for this free-thinking theatre, founded in 1976. Today, behind the now iconic building soars an overhead motorway, sending cars streaming south-west to Soweto and north to the once white suburbs and beyond. Beneath the roar sits acres of old buildings reassigned to new use as craft markets, dance-cum-recording-cum-playmaking studios and dusty cafes. It's now trendy instead of depressed.

Once it stood among much more desolate surroundings, a few dinky shops nestling nearby, selling dubious Africana to apartheid tourists, several grubby pubs and a jazz club called Kippy's. In the theatre's precinct the paving bore brass platelets with the names of donors, which have long since vanished, just the tiny shallow graves remaining. Gone together with the copper wiring that any self-respecting thief could nick from the sidings nearby. Or from anywhere, in fact, throughout the land. Hence South Africa's matchless telephone-wire basketry, a craft perfected by poverty.

This theatre, famous for its protest plays during the apartheid years, sailed close to the wind until liberation in 1994. Then, once the enemy had gone, it lost its way. It's beginning to find it again, under the new directorship of James Ncgobo, so it's with a gusty sigh of relief that I can offer up a brief picture of the censorship it once had to face, where, thankfully, there is none anymore. Well, not thus far in theatres – although newspapers are hotting up as the next battleground, but that's another story.

In those dark days, the censor's office would act if an individual made a complaint in writing, having been present at a play, and, however silly the complaint, the board would need to follow it up. The Market was then left with the appeal process and picking up the pieces of a damaged run, all very costly. Banning orders were served on five or six plays, mainly between 1976 and 1980.

The first to be banned was Comedians by Trevor Griffiths, accused of bad language and blasphemy, with lawyer Ernest Wentzel defending the play. The hearing meandered on for four-and-a-half hours, the prosecution argument being that the use of slang and expletives was down to a "paucity of vocabulary". At a certain point, an impatient chairman repaired to his office with the directorate and weird bargaining then

ABOVE: Sarafina, written and directed by Mbongeni Ngema, at the Market Theatre in 1987. The musical tells the story of students involved in anti-apartheid protests, inspired by the 1976 Soweto riots

ensued, along the lines of whether the Market CEO Mannie Manim would "forgo the 'c-word' on page five in order to retain the 'f-word' on page seven". This was negotiated throughout the text until enough of it was left to continue the run – with the author's bemused permission. All in all, it was a win, as the production was not forced to close and the theatre benefited from the surge of publicity. Best of all, the negotiations served as fodder for stand-up satirists.

After this victory, the Market, under the aegis of Manim, developed the argument that the appeal board should see the performance in question as the audience sees it, and so after each banning order he would call the chairman of the board and request one more performance, after which the appeal could be heard in the auditorium itself, where the play had been performed. With surprising fairness, the censor agreed to this. A full house – of everyone's best friends, of course – would be asked to attend the special performance.

I recall a peach of a situation when a complaint was registered against Spike Milligan and John Atrobus's daft comedy The Bed-Sitting Room, which was banned on →

→ two counts: one for blasphemy in that God was portrayed as an old man wandering around in striped pyjamas, and secondly for cannibalism in that a talking parrot called Harold Macmillan fell off his perch and was duly roasted and eaten. A magistrate was called out (I could swear still in his own striped pyjamas) at 11pm one night and the special performance was duly given, to gales of laughter, and then the hearing went ahead after the performance. Raymond Tucker, the Market's lawyer, won the case that night, though there were many nail-biting moments when it proved difficult to keep a straight face.

Another banning, called Holy Moses and All That Jazz, a children's musical based on Bible stories, was defended by a lawyer

When I directed Othello – a play about race and sex if ever there was one – no bans were served, even after the sensational onstage kiss

called Denis Kuny, who was a bass player in his spare time. The major premise of the banning was the title; the censors held that association with "jazz" denigrated Moses. You have to remember that we were living under Calvinist rule, our leaders a brace of Bible-thumpers. When it became clear that the Market was heading for another victory, the chairman of the appeal board asked Kuny if the theatre could please consider another title without the word "jazz". Which is when Kuny launched into a short history of the great musical art form, to waves of applause from the audience. When he turned dramatically to the board at the end of his highly informed peroration, the chairman had to concede that the case was won.

Those who made the complaints were usually out to cause havoc to the Market willy-

nilly, but here's the surprise: very few of the political and "in-your-face" protest plays were ever censored. Powerful pieces that were staged without interference included The Island; Sizwe Banzi is Dead; Statements after an Arrest Under the Immorality Act; Miss Julie (the white actress Sandra Prinsloo needed armed bodyguards to escort her from the theatre); Woza Albert!; Asinamali!; Born in the RSA; You Strike the Woman, You Strike the Rock; The Sun Will Rise (the most outspoken piece of revolutionary "drama" the Market ever presented, by poets Matsemela Manaka, Maishe Maponya and Ingoapele Madingoane). Oh, and many others. The audience for these was the core of liberal Johannesburg, eager to seek solace in their guilt-assuaging, anti-establishment theatre.

My own view is that the complainants were too, shall we say, limited to realise that satire is a dangerous tool. And not only satire, high tragedy too. When I directed Othello in 1986-87 – a play about race and sex if ever there was one – no bans were served, even after the sensational onstage kiss between the black lead, John Kani, and blonder-than-blonde Joanna Weinberg. Never mind that seats banged up as affronted white couples left in protest, not a dicky bird of a banning was to be heard. Threatening letters galore, yes, and cross-looking cops in the precinct. But Shakespeare – bless him – was never listed as a bannable person under any sub-clause in any legal act. And is one surprised? I mean, who would dare?

I rather bank on the fact that what I have described above will seem somewhat infantile to readers, and for me these distant memories highlight an almost absurdist attitude to the regime's priorities, which led to John Kani driving daily to Othello rehearsals from his home in Soweto wearing two T-shirts, the top one covering his black-green-yellow ANC one, in case a cop stopped him en route.

However, to be truthful, although you had to laugh – what my grandmother called a bitter laugh – it wasn't so funny at the time, because stupidity can be cruel and it can wreak vengeance.

An incident comes to mind that might well highlight the almost childish delight one took in making that stupidity appear stupider: in the 60s, London boasted a splendiferous world theatre season under the direction of the late Sir Peter Daubeney, and funded by The Sunday Times. A South African company was invited to present their Zulu-ised Macbeth, a sensationally exciting version of the play, performed by a huge company, directed by Welcome Msomi, which received rapturous notices. One day Msomi phoned and asked me how I thought the company should respond as he had received a formal invitation from the South African ambassador to come to the embassy in Trafalgar Square for a reception in their honour.

But, that embassy building was terra non grata, not to say incognita. No self-respecting South African would set foot in it while the nationalists governed. Outside it, in Trafalgar Square, were permanent anti-apartheid vigils. I had never entered its portals. For the uMabatha Company to refuse the invitation might have been imprudent; no nation likes bad publicity and they had to go home after the run, and then who knows? He and I came to the conclusion that the company should accept, but make very sure that Nkosi Sikelel' iAfrika (the then banned anthem of the ANC, and now the lead anthem of a free South Africa) should somehow be sung by the company during the course of the proceedings in that hallowed building.

And that's what happened. At what we thought seemed an appropriate moment, after many speeches, the full company of Zulus rose shyly to their feet and the tear-making beauty of African part-singing rose in great sonorous waves to the gilded Lutyens ceiling. Horror! The revolutionary song within the sacred sanctum of Afrikanerdom! *Die swart gevaar* (the black peril) had breached the walls! I shan't forget

ABOVE: Othello, directed by Janet Suzman in 1986, with John Kani in the lead and Joanna Weinberg as Desdemona

the expressions on the faces of the rows of embassy staffers, who, with their crimplene-clad wives were forced to rise to their feet, par politesse, eyes swiveling nervously towards their grey-suited spouses, who were staring sternly straight ahead, quelling panic.

Since that small triumph I have considered that presence rather than absence is the more telling form of protest. I remember playwright Athol Fugard changing his mind about a cultural boycott of South Africa, having in the first place persuaded the likes of Peter Hall and Harold Pinter that a boycott must be instigated. I, too, changed →

→ my mind when I would go back to South Africa year after year and see how much the absence of ideas, of argument, was pleasing to the regime. Silence gave them nothing to worry about. Except for those troublesome actors down at the Market, life was fairly peaceful. Which was why, in 1987, I decided to break the Equity boycott by directing the production of Othello. I was a rookie, but I thought the subject more crucial than my inexperience, and luckily John Kani agreed. The story of a black man being humiliated by a white thug, written in the highest poetry a mind can imagine, seemed to us the perfect metaphorical mechanism for disturbing the peace, and having persuaded the ANC culture-desk-in-exile that Shakespeare was a protest playwright of the first water, so

The sleepy old Cape is host to some hard-hitting, post-apartheid writing

it proved. It hardly needs saying that cultural – I shall include academic – boycotts hurt those you least want to hurt, whereas economic and, in the case of South Africa, sports boycotts reach the ones who remain smug about what they're part of.

Here's a nice paradox: an angry young black man rises to his feet at a political meeting before the second democratic elections – when still, as now, nothing much had been delivered to the poor – and he brandishes his fist and shouts: "We fought for freedom and look what we got! Democracy!" So you may say that South Africa remains as paradoxical as ever; no censorship per se but a darkening new Protection of State Information Bill, commonly known as the secrecy act, that threatens to jeopardise South Africa's long treasured free press. It's what President Jacob Zuma desires – he doesn't like appearing in cartoons with a shower attachment growing out of his head and other such absurdi-

ties. After 20 years of freedom, the Market cannot be given more importance than it deserves, as, happily, it's not the only theatre offering up food for thought. On the contrary, its new artistic director will have to do what all directors worldwide have to do: find a balanced programme that will pull in the punters. New work, old work and lots of fun to attract the young. Though, after all these years, I still have to confess to a thrill of real delight that this artistic director is black – a youth spent in South Africa dies hard, I fear.

Indeed, theatre may not be the toothiest place to bare your protest fangs; the streets and the public squares of the world are in a perpetual tumult of Twitter. Egypt and Ukraine have made the front pages, as the people forge their destiny. Yet, censors still crack down on playwrights in Turkey, Lebanon and many other countries. But, when allowed to function without state interference, the theatre remains the one orderly forum where you freely choose to plant your butt to take part in an attempt at understanding the world. Very Athenian. Once upon a time, when Athol Fugard started writing, it was the Space Theatre in Cape Town that sent his plays northwards to Johannesburg's Market. Now that's in reverse. The sleepy old Cape is host to some hard-hitting, post-apartheid writing.

At the Baxter Theatre, on the University of Cape Town (UCT) campus, the director, Lara Foot is a dynamo who has instigated an annual arts festival – Zabalaza – to celebrate black playmaking, and which explodes every March. She writes up a storm, too. Her most triumphant play, Tshepang, which deals with the horror of baby rape, has recently caused a mighty ruckus by being incorporated into a school exam syllabus, with a bald, out-of-context question causing a huge fuss.

Interestingly, arty Afrikaners flock to their own cultural fests at Oudshoorn and elsewhere so the language can show itself off without flinching – a beleaguered tribe on the back foot but aching to get on the front one. It's a very expressive language and it possesses wonderful writers – Reza de Wet, Antjie Krog, André Brink spring to mind. The Fugard Theatre, on the fringe of District Six and founded by South African expat Eric Abraham, is presenting a newly commissioned play by Nicholas Wright, which harks back to the old era. Based on a true story, it tells of Pumla Gobodo-Madikizela's work as a psychologist and her extended interviews in prison with Eugene de Kock, a cop so murderous he is known as Prime Evil. The dramatisation examines, with some shock, her feelings of unexpected sympathy for the man, and the play will run in London later this year.

The university town of Grahamstown, always on a knife-edge of financial meltdown, hosts its excitements through July's National Arts Fest, where the fringe is nigh as rich as Edinburgh's. There's plenty of new writing there – some good, some bad.

The country is traumatised, yes, but it is traumatised in 11 languages and many races. That makes for a rich mix. We seek and we toil for excellence and sometimes we find it. I am forever on the look out and have lately been entranced with a new piece that has played Johannesburg, Cape Town and Edinburgh, and which London will see in the autumn. It's called Solomon and Marion and yet again the multi-talented Lara Foot has to take her place as a leading playwright in the new South Africa with this one. I am in it and it seems to me a particularly South African genesis for a piece of playwrighting.

Ripple-dissolve to 2006 and a large company of actors is rehearsing Hamlet in a taped-up, mock-up of the Swan Theatre, Stratford in the women's residence at UCT. Easter weekend is upon us, and we are fighting fit, having just completed what I, as director, considered a terrific run-through. Give the cast a break until Monday night, I say, and on Thursday we fly to the UK for the 'big adventure'. We had been invited by the Royal Shakespeare Company to open their international Complete Works Festival, a singular honour. Excitement ran high. But one of us, a young man called Brett Goldin, playing Guildenstern, would not see Shakespeare's birthplace, would never have his dream. He was murdered that weekend by two thugs in Cape Town, high on tik-tik, as crystal meth is known.

This fatal tragic event has fed into the mind of a writer and come out years later as a beautiful play. It's both comedic and cathartic and, although I wish Brett's life were not the price for it, I am astonished at how joyous trauma can become. That, one can but hope, is the future for South Africa. Another paradox. ⊠

© Janet Suzman
www.indexoncensorship.org

IIIIIIIIIIIIIIIIIIIIIIIIIIIIIIIIIIIIIIIIIIIIIIIIIIII

Brief biography

Janet Suzman was born in Johannesburg in 1939.

After moving to the UK in 1959, she trained at the London Academy of Music and Dramatic Art. She became a member of the Royal Shakespeare Company in 1963, going on to play many of Shakespeare's greatest heroines.

Her leading role in Nicholas and Alexandra in 1971 earned her a nomination for the Academy Award for Best Actress.

She also appeared in many British television productions, including 1986 BBC drama The Singing Detective.

In the late 1990s, she toured with her adaptation of Chekhov's The Cherry Orchard, set in post-apartheid South Africa and called The Free State.

She is the niece of Helen Suzman (1917–2009), the prominent anti-apartheid campaigner who was twice nominated for the Nobel Peace Prize.

Big men, big decisions

43(2): 164/169 | DOI: 10.1177/0306422014534154

Novelist **Christie Watson** writes a powerful new short story for Index, set against a backdrop of the recent anti-gay legislation in Nigeria

❚❚❚ BELIEVE FICTION ALLOWS us truth: to see humanity, and sometimes (a rather terrifying) reflection of ourselves," says author Christie Watson of her short story, You are a Big Man, the story of a bombastic and self-absorbed Nigerian politician responsible for passing a harsh new law against homosexuality.

Written for Index on Censorship magazine and published here for the first time, the tale takes its inspiration from the country's recently enforced anti-gay legislation. Although gay sex has long been illegal in the country, January saw an unprecedented crackdown. Same-sex marriage became illegal, under secular as well as sharia law, with a penalty of up to 14 years in prison. A "public show" of same-sex relations also carries the risk of a long jail term, as does participation in gay organisations, or a simple show of support.

Against this backdrop of increasing persecution, with violent vigilantes hunting down transgressors, author Christie Watson decided to return her attention to the country that remains close to her heart. Nigeria is the setting for Watson's first novel, Tiny Sunbirds Far Away, written from the perspective of a 12-year-old girl in the Niger delta, which won the Costa first-book award in 2011.

"As I started to think about motivations behind the politics [of the anti-gay laws], I wanted to explore the idea of distraction," she tells Index of her latest story. In You are a Big Man, the protagonist's stream-of-consciousness shows an inability to focus on the country's major issues, as his mind is pulled to thoughts of luxury goods, sex and his own power. "I originally wrote it from a third person point-of-view," Watson tells Index. "But then I played around with the idea of second person: the idea that the world is watching the 'you' in the story."

"What's on your mind?" asks the politician's wife, presuming her husband is waking in the night with thoughts of a boarding-school massacre, similar to a real life tragedy at Buni Yadi secondary school in February when 59 pupils were killed by gunmen from Islamist group Boko Haram. "That too," he says, before revealing the main cause of his night sweats: the responsibility of "regulating" gay people.

Watson says: "I'm so saddened by what's happening in Nigeria now. I used to hold much hope for the country's future, and I still have hope, but now, and particularly in the run up to 2015 elections, the immediate future looks bleak."

YOU ARE A Big Man.

You are a big man in Abuja.

You fly a different girlfriend to Dubai every weekend, and distribute made-to-order Louboutins around the place like leaflets. You are generous. Gifts of $100,000. You are responsible for so many women.

You are a gifted polo player, have an accomplished political career and billions of dollars stashed in offshore accounts.

You are God-fearing.

So what is it keeping you awake? Giving headaches? There is no ibuprofen, only paracetamol, and it vexes you, this small thing, and I see you sit up on to pillows, and rub your temples until your wife, sleeping soundly, begins to snore. "Are you awake?" Your voice like a little boy's, like one of her boys. "I have pain."

Her eyes slowly open, bloodshot, filled with sleep. Old, tired eyes. Behind her a photograph on the nightstand of four children: three boys, one girl. The most handsome of the boys, Dayo, staring away from the camera at something distant. Or someone. Who?

"Where's the ibuprofen? You said you'd source some. There's a big meeting tomorrow. It's important. I can't sleep."

She breathes deeply. "What is it?" Her voice soft and measured. Practised. "What's on your mind?" Her breath is sour, stale, old. You think of a girlfriend who keeps a pack of mints underneath the pillow so that she can freshen her mouth anytime you want to kiss it.

"Ungodly. All of them."

Your wife sits up, strokes your back, her hand rough. "Those poor children. The families."

ABOVE: Christie Watson

"That, too. Of course, that! It is completely immoral. Disgusting. And I can't sleep."

"You need some paracetamol?"

"Above all, a man like me needs sleep."

"I'll get some."

"Do you have any idea what it is like, thinking about gays and their behaviour? Regulating them? Trying to bring such evil to the forefront of public consciousness? Sleep. And ibufrofen," you say, shaking her off. "The 400mgs." The burning spreads down, a hand-pressing skull. Then you turn, grab her face, squeeze her cheeks until her mouth becomes a perfect O. You push her head down away from your face, to your lap.

The driver has kept the car cool by running the air-conditioning full but it is →

sweltering even so. As soon as you climb into the car, trousers stick to the leather seat. "This car is getting shabby. But no matter. I've recently ordered – not one but how many? – state-of-the-art, bulletproof BMWs. I need them. I've sacrificed my safety for my country. And you, you are a lucky driver."

A child of 10 years old bangs on the window. "Quicker," you shout. The child's hands starfish against the glass: dry peeling skin, scabs, bloody. Open. Listening. An image of children glows in front of you: murdered in their boarding-school beds. You force it away. It is your responsibility to force such images away. "There's no fight in these people." You talk. "Nigeria. More out-of-school children than anywhere in the world they say, and yet here look. How can you blame us, when these people have no fight themselves."

The driver winds down the partition.

"Sorry sir, I could not hear you."

"They do nothing for themselves." The smell of the sweat of the driver dances around. "This is unhygienic. How can you come for a day's work without first showering? There is a long list of drivers who would gladly take your job."

The partition falls down a fraction. "Sorry, sir." The driver's eyes glance in the mirror. His shirt dirty, dark patches of grime on the collar. "Sorry, sir. We have had no power for five days. No water. No electricity."

"I find that hard to believe. Anyway, you need to save for a generator. You're not some hawker at the side of a road but my personal driver. You have the kind of smell that clings

to fabric. I have the executive president's ear. Do you think I can speak into the president's ear smelling like a sewer rat? Get your house in order."

"Yes, sir. I am doing my best, sir."

"Do you think anyone cares if you sleep?"

"Sorry, sir?"

This is what is inside you:

Your headache is gone but in its place is a feeling of restlessness. Your responsibilities are too big. Legislating immorality is your duty. Protecting people. And winning the 2015 election is your responsibility. Whatever it takes. Distraction. Later today you will call a girlfriend, or maybe send for a new girl – or two. Powerful men have powerful needs.

"We have been likened to Nazis." The young woman's voice fills the room and is followed with quiet that moves between the three men, twisting in seats.

You stand, walk to the silver cabinet adorned with gold leaf and aluminium, and lift the heavy embossed lid to find the cognac. You fill a gold-leaf-trimmed glass almost to the top, let the vapours travel up, breathe deeply. "This is good stuff."

Godwin laughs until his enormous stomach shakes almost independently of his body. His shining face has tiny sweat-beads. "Only the best." He turns to the young woman. "What else are they saying? Read out the comments. Would you like to try this cognac while you read? It's the best cognac in the world."

She shakes her head, looks at the papers on her lap. Sighs. She wears dark trousers and a white blouse that is not quite, but nearly transparent. You imagine her in her underwear, without her underwear.

ABOVE: Gay-rights protesters outside the Nigerian embassy in London in February, after Nigeria passed its law against homosexuality

"One of the comments on Twitter," she reads. "'They took time to sign a bill into law for being gay? I don't have electricity'." And another, "'Our president is covering up incompetence with hatred of gays: meanwhile Boko Haram kill another 300 this month. Shine your eyes, Nigeria.'" She shuffles papers, looks around the room. Follow her eyes. Three important men. Members of the National Assembly. Your friends. Great thinkers like you.

"There are rumours already," she says.

"What are you talking about?"

She swallows loudly enough that you hear it and focus on her slim throat. I see inside you. You think: I want to hold her throat while I fuck her. Then, God, the pain in your head. As if someone is crushing your skull.

"There's gossip among the politically active community. Rumours. But the sources are wide and trustworthy. About a list." She crosses and uncrosses her legs. "They say there's a list. A long list."

"What list?" You flick your arm and a splash of cognac falls on the marble floor.

"Don't waste too much of that," Godwin laughs. "It is worth $200,000."

"You have the most expensive tastes of anyone I know."

Solomon lifts his long arm, his thin fingers wrapped around the glass, brings it to his face and looks through it until his usually perfectly shaped head is surreal and distorted. "Beauté du Siècle. Only a few bottles left in existence."

The young woman sits upright, lifts her long neck. "The list," she says. Her voice is louder. "They say there is a list of gay men and women who are all the offspring of the NASS members."

Silence. Your heart so quiet it feels as though it's stopped beating. Vision blurred. You try and sharpen it, focus on objects: the surrealist art on the wall, Solomon's distorted head, the statues, the solid gold table holding photographs of Godwin's family – his wife on their yacht in Monaco, her Hermès scarf blowing around her face, his racehorses, lined up one by one, his daughter who is in Germany being treated for toothache. She, unmarried at 37, living in LA. Solomon's son: in London, whispers, whispers, whispers. Your reflection in a gold-trimmed glass. Bloated and dull.

"Nonsense," Godwin laughs from where he sits on one of the Italian leather sofas, his stretched out naked feet, toes squeaking on the polished marble floor. "This young girl is an expert in managing social media but what does she know of political matters?"

She falls further into the armchair.

"It's good to have a young female social media adviser among us. Especially after the incident before. But let's leave the official talk for later." Godwin shifts back but his eyes remain on the girl. "Manage the Twitter account and I'll review things later." Godwin waves until she stands. A curtain of fat moves underneath his arm. "Privately," he says, winking and grinning widely.

"They say this law is dangerous. And people have been killed already and many, many more will be killed," she says, before leaving the room, her court shoes tapping, tapping, tapping.

She is not afraid. You see that and feel longing.

"Opponents will argue it violates human rights but people don't understand the law. Fundamental human rights are not an absolute."

"It's a question of morality." Solomon's glass drops from his face. "We don't need homosexuality and Aids here! Here in Nigeria we've passed laws in line with our own cultural and religious inclinations. Nigerians are pleased with it. These haters are few. Let them shout. We're the lawmakers and we speak for our people. Let us extricate ourselves from the West. We have new friends. Do you know what those people are doing with their anus? It's disgusting."

Godwin yawns. "It's a good distraction from the NNPC thing."

"I've been suffering headaches," you say. "All those billion dollars' worth of missing receipts," you say, touching your temples. "Children slaughtered."

"Hell." Cognac swigged, then glass re-filled.

"Pressure," you say, touching the top of your skull. "And down the back."

"Receipts are easy to find, my friend. And you know what I think? All this discussion is being hampered by these basic needs we have as men. Call up those girls," says Solomon. "We'll send the cars, clear the roads: they should be here soon. All these stirrings in my loins are causing a distraction from important matters. I need to drink, to fuck, then eat. In that order!"

"Great men have great needs," you say.

After all, you are among friends. These men, like you, are great men. Of course you all let off steam now and then to help solve the complexities of Nigeria; it's in the nation's interest. Nigeria's interest. There's an election coming. And you have things to distract people from. This law will make you popular. Win votes. It's a huge responsibility. You are godly men, proud men. The future of Nigeria. Together you make laws protecting Nigeria from immorality. From Aids. No one knows the headaches you bear. The pain of making these decisions. You sit down on the leather sofa, on top of the darkness. Godwin and Solomon click their glasses against yours. You smile. You drink the cognac quickly, wait for girls. Drink, eat, fuck. Drink, eat, fuck. Drink, eat, fuck. ◪

©Christie Watson
www.indexoncensorship.org

All characters in this work are fictitious.

Christie Watson is a British novelist. Her second book, Where Women Are Kings, was published in October. She tweets @tinysunbird

"The exiled poet, free once more"

43(2): 170/175 | DOI: 10.1177/0306422014534152

Poet and author Lev Ozerov was one of the most important literary figures documenting the suffering of Ukrainian Jews in the Holocaust. But he is yet to win due recognition, says translator and poet **Robert Chandler**. Here, Chandler writes an introduction to his own translation of Ozerov's poem Zabolotsky, pubished here for the first time in English

BORN IN KIEV in 1914, Lev Ozerov worked as a frontline journalist during World War II. After the liberation of Kiev, Ozerov was commissioned to write an article for The Black Book (a documentary account of the Shoah on Soviet soil) about the massacre of Jews carried out by the Nazis at Babi Yar, a ravine just outside the city. The Black Book was published decades later, but Ozerov's long poem about Babi Yar – judged by literary scholar Maxim Shrayer to be "the most historically reliable and extensive treatment of Babi Yar in all of Soviet poetry" – was published in 1946.

From 1943, Ozerov worked as a teacher, translator and critic. He did much to enable the publication of writers who had suffered or perished under Stalin and was the first editor to publish Russian poet Nikolay Zabolotsky on his return from the Gulag in 1946.

Ozerov has yet to win due recognition. His finest book, Portraits Without Frames, (published posthumously in 1999) constitutes a mini-encyclopedia of Soviet culture; it comprises 50 accounts, told with deceptive simplicity, of meetings with important figures, many – though not all – from the literary world. One poem tells how Yevgenia Taratuta, an editor of children's literature, kept her sanity during brutal interrogations by reciting Pushkin and Mayakovsky to herself. A lighter poem tells of Boris Slutsky's generosity in making his room available to couples who had nowhere to sleep together; one evening he returns home to find a note: "Boris, / you are a great humanist, / and the heavenly powers / will reward you. The sins of others, / sins that are not yours, / will bring you blessings." The subjects of other portraits include Babel; Platonov; Shostakovich; Tatlin; the ballet dancer Galina Ulanova; and Kovpak, a Ukrainian partisan leader.

Zabolotsky

'What do I need?'
'Trousers, of course.
Doesn't matter if they're old,
or who's worn them before.
They need to be strong –
that's all.
My own have fallen to bits.
And put some tobacco,
the very cheapest,
in the pockets.'
So Nikolay Zabolotsky
conversed with himself,
about to send a letter to his wife
in the year 1940.
He was in Komsomolsk,
on the river Amur.
Even in this hell
he knew moments of triumph.
On the radio he once heard
a few stanzas from The Knight in the Tiger Skin
by Shota Rustaveli.
Heavens! Was he hearing right?
No mention of the translator,
a poet who'd been sent to the camps.
Like it or not, he mastered
a few different crafts.
All came in handy:
patience, silence, competence,
competence, deftness, silence.
'Humble yourself, proud man!'
– yes, Fyodor Mikhailovich,
that can stand you in good stead.
It's good advice.
If you want to speak,
keep silent.
There are ears everywhere,
ears and more ears.

ABOVE: Lev Ozerov

And like it or not,
you must remember:
to keep silent in your cell,
to keep silent in the column,
to keep silent in the quarry.
It's better to listen.
And if a word
tries to escape you,
don't help it out.
First an inbreath,
then an outbreath.
And it's over.
No, it's not over.

Like it or not,
one learns
to mistrust man,
to mistrust the word.
Keep silent, but not even silence
will always help.
It's crowded in the cattle truck.
It's dark in the cattle truck.
It's terribly cold –
and there's nothing to eat.
Only black,
soot-covered icicles –
prisoners' popsicles,
cattle-truck toffee.
Worse still
is having to meet
the stare of a criminal
who wants to hit you with a log.
'They've given me 10 years.
And now I'm going to smash you.
Smash you hard.'
And there he was,
right in front of Zabolotsky,
about to do away with
some bespectacled intellectual.
His mates got in the way:
'Calm down, brother – not now!'
Salvation
brings joy to the heart.
Within an hour
the lines had composed themselves.
Heavens, who knows anything
of the paths of poetry?
'Forest Lake' – who could have imagined it?
Composed in a stinking,
crowded cattle-truck.
So much
for Mount Olympus.
Later, when we met,

he never said one word
about the camps.
The master of the high style
was taciturn, slow
to respond, as if
he were short of words.
How very little he said.
And how fiercely he hated
our native braggarts.
I first met Zabolotsky
only when he returned from the camps.
He was considered a goner,
but his family needed him
and his friends needed him
and literature needed him.
'Greetings, Nikolay Alexeyevich!'
A pause, a half smile,
and he quietly held out his hand.
That was easier for him
than saying words.
Words for him
had a different purpose.
'Have you written anything new?'
I asked cautiously.
A long pause,
a pause that went on so long
I began to feel awkward
about having asked.
'No!' he said in the end,
sadly and in confusion.
And out of habit
I got to my feet and said loudly,
'Amid these miracles, amid these living plants,
why seek new storms and new impressions?
Breathe the imperfect wisdom of this land,
O soul that never tires of questions.'
Zabolotsky listened
and remarked, as if by the way,
'A poem. The title's Lodeinikov.'

'Yes, I know. Your Second Book.
Please allow me to read more.'
And I went on reciting,
without his permission,
shouting, working myself into a frenzy,
pacing up and down the room.
There was the breath of the North
in his poems, and the breath
of the South, the life of a market,
the life of a football field.
The exiled poet was free once more;
and he was listening to his own poems
as if they'd been written by someone else,
as if just recovered
from some safe hiding place.
I exhausted
the stores of my memory
and Zabolotsky went on his way.
That evening
he said to his daughter
over a cup of tea,
'I thought I'd been quite forgotten,
but it seems people still remember me.'
I learned this only recently,
several decades after this meeting.
I heard this from Natalya Nikolayevna,
the poet's daughter. ⊠

Translated by Robert Chandler

Robert Chandler's translations from Russian include Vasily Grossman's Everything Flows, The Road, and Life and Fate. He has compiled two Penguin Classics anthologies on Russian short stories and Russian magic tales. A third anthology, The Penguin Book of Russian Poetry, will include several more poems by Lev Ozerov and will be published this November

Ghost of Turkey's past

43(2): 176/185 | DOI: 10.1177/0306422014534153

On the 50th anniversary of Turkish writer Halide Edip Adivar's death, novelist **Kaya Genç** writes a haunting tale about this controversial figure

"IT HAD TO be a ghost story," says Istanbul-based novelist Kaya Genç of his short story, To Tell, Or Not To Tell, published here for the first time. Set in Istanbul University's literature faculty, it takes the idea of the department's founder returning from the dead to speak to those who she feels should be safeguarding her reputation.

Born in 1884, Halide Edip Adıvar became a renowned feminist leader and a key figure in Turkish nationalism in the early 1920s. She was fiercely intellectual, incredibly well-read and worked tirelessly for girls to gain equal education opportunities. Yet Genç believes she has been maligned by male historians, who painted her as a traitor. In 1926, after she fell out with the leaders of the new republican regime about the direction the revolution should take, she was accused of treason and fled to Europe. Adıvar believed too much power had been laid in the hands of too few men. She wanted more political representation for women and a more horizontal and democratic power structure," says Genç.

This year marks the 50th anniversary of Adıvar's death and, although some universities marked the occassion with honorary events, the wider public paid no heed. "This is, unfortunately, the fate of authors in Turkey," says Genç. "People love to ignore figures who don't have radical political beliefs. Adıvar was a democrat and wanted moderation in the political sphere. This was enough to get her into trouble during her lifetime."

Genç, who studied for a literature doctorate at Istanbul University, says he was inspired to write the story for Index after seeing Adıvar's old chair in the head of department's office two years ago. In his story, Adıvar directs her attentions towards a middle-aged female scholar, who feels under pressure from a different sort of repression as she struggle to contain her own secrets and beliefs. "One has to speak out," Adıvar warns her. "When you start speaking out, it turns into a kind of habit." Such advice seems all the more pertinent after the Turkish goverment's recent crackdown on social networks, including Twitter and YouTube.

Genç says he first started to read about Adıvar's controversial past when he was a first year at college and his own tutors were more forthright when discussing her. "In Turkey, university administrations are generally suspicious of English literature departments. They worry that those departments may introduce dangerous ideas to their pupils. This was one of the reasons I liked being there. We had sparky tutors and their discussions on feminism made a lasting impression on me."

ABOVE: Students outside Istanbul University's main entrance on Beyazit Square

He hopes the story might spark some interest in feminist Turkish writers and highly recommends Adıvar's Memoirs and her novel The Clown and His Daughter, about a young girl's relationship with her father who plays the female role in the *oyunu* (the orta), traditional Turkish theatre.

To Tell, Or Not To Tell

The long corridor of the department of Western literatures was dimmed. They walked silently, as if not wanting to raise the dead. They passed pictures of classic authors, hung on the long, white wall. She knew them by heart: Faulkner, Nabokov, London, Hemingway and Woolf. Men accompanied by a woman, placed there as if to prevent female scholars from complaining of sexism. He took a bronze key and placed it into the lock of the second door from the left. The door opened with a wooden sound.

"But this is her room," she whispered. "We can't do it here."

He closed the door, double-locked it, held her waist, lifted and placed her body on the metal desk.

Although it was darker here, her inner eye reminded her what was inside. When she pushed aside a pile of papers, she instinctively knew they were article abstracts handed in by graduate students earlier in the day. Her body landed on a book, which she identified as the Oxford Shakespeare, and she threw it of the way, on to the wooden chair adjacent to the desk.

→ His fingers ran across her body. She imagined herself from outside: a woman in her 40s, sitting half-naked on her boss's desk.

"Someone may come inside," she whispered, although she knew it was impossible.

"Inside," she repeated. "Someone can come."

She remembered the first time she had laid eyes on him. It couldn't have been more than a month ago when he had arrogantly entered the assistants' room, asking if they had "proper coffee". She closed her eyes and

She asked them to forget the things they learned in high school, because most of that was inaccurate

allowed him to do whatever he liked and when something entered the room a minute later, her eyes were half-open.

She saw a shadow move on the wall. It belonged to neither of them and had the distinct outline of a woman who was coming towards them like some strange butterfly.

"Shakespeare," the ghost whispered. "How thoughtful of you to have placed Shakespeare's works on my old wooden chair. Thank you! The Bard had been my favourite author since girls' school. He was a very passionate fellow, you know, and I am sure he would be very happy to watch you at this late hour, making love in a room wrongly rumoured to have once belonged to me..."

She looked at this presence, which had an outline but not a proper body, and it sent shivers down her spine.

"This is impossible," he said. His sentence had stood up with him as he raised his body to her shoulder level. "I know you. You are Halide Edip Adıvar. You died 50 years ago... You are dead!"

The ghost came closer and it was as if it had the power to change any historical fact she desired. Its self-assurance scared her. She wished she were in bed with her husband, and imagined her daughter lying safely in her room. Instead she was in Halide Edip Adıvar's room, talking to her ghost – without wearing any underwear.

She looked at Halide's ghost. She had black eyelashes, a strong nose, and the lips of an angry woman. Her hair was cut short.

"Why are you here?" she asked. "Is it because you are mad at us?"

"Maybe I am mad at you. Maybe I hate you. Maybe I am here to teach you a lesson."

He made it to the door and turned on the lights. As the fluorescent lamps lit, one by one, she listened to their sounds and, when she looked at the room again, she realised that Halide was gone.

* * *

Who was Halide? She was the founder of their department, perhaps the biggest feminist icon in Turkey's early republican history, and a political exile whose troubled life she had once written about in a much-discussed article. Earlier in the day, during an orientation meeting with freshman students in the large faculty hall, her name had come up and it was only after seeing her ghost that she realised the connection.

It had been a very short meeting. Some pupils had brought coffee to class; a stylishly dressed girl had played with her iPad Mini throughout. At least two boys had dozed in the solitude of the back seats.

"A very good morning and semester to you," she had told them.

"As this is your first class at university, perhaps I should remind you that you are no longer in high school. University is another country. We do things differently here."

She had asked them to forget all the things they had learned in high school because, unfortunately, most of that was inaccurate, thanks to the ideological nature of Turkish historiography. She had scribbled a few words on the board – Halide's name among them – and had told them about the department head and the professors and the assistants and office hours and other practical details. But it had been Halide's name that had attracted the pupils' interest most. The skinny girl with the tablet computer had raised her hand.

"Can you tell us about Halide Edip Adıvar and the history of the department?"

"Well, you have answered your own question. Halide Edip Adıvar's life is the very history of our department."

"In other words, ours is a traitorous department," a voice had said from the crowd.

"Who said that?"

"I did," an attractive young man had said. "I remember learning in high school that Halide Edip Adıvar was a traitor and sold the country to Americans."

"And did they tell you how much she was paid?"

"I heard she was against the republic and that was why she was exiled to London,"

ABOVE: Halide Edip Adıvar, on a Turkish stamp, circa 1966

another voice from the back said. "She was too scared to return to Istanbul because she was a renegade."

"This is your high-school education speaking," she had managed to say, taken aback by the comments. But she had dropped the matter because it had been a tiring day, and she had been too busy thinking about him and about his remark about "meeting up" after the final class. So she left the Halide discussion to a later date. "If you took note of office hours and the address of our Facebook page, then that will be enough for the day," she had said.

* * *

The morning after Halide had appeared in the head of department's room, they →

stood next to the water cooler to prepare coffee. It had been their morning ritual for the past three weeks. When they stood there they could flirt as much and unashamedly as they liked. He asked her how she had slept the previous night.

"Not very well, as you can imagine. It was the sleep someone would have after seeing a ghost."

"I think I know the feeling."

"We should tell the head of department what happened."

"Is that what you think? We should tell her that, while her new assistant was mak-

This time she looked older, with a monocle on her face and a cigarette hanging out of her mouth. It was scarier to meet her alone

ing out with an assistant professor on her desk, the ghost of Halide Edip Adıvar had come inside and caught them in the act? That would give her a perfect reason to fire both of us, would it not?"

"But she has a right to know," she said, putting sugar in her cup. "What if she has a similar experience? That could give her a heart attack and we would regret it for the rest of our lives."

"I don't think I would care much for her health if she fires me," he said. Then he came near her and touched her arm and pressed his body on to hers. She said nothing but wanted to resist him and thought keeping silent would be a means of doing that, but he did not back off.

* * *

She took the coffee with her to class where she came across some of the faces she had seen the previous day. Not all of them were here, but those who talked about Halide were.

"Yesterday," she began, "I mentioned some practical details about our department."

"Namely that it was founded by a traitor," the attractive boy said automatically.

"Haha!" The skinny girl laughed.

"I have to say that is also how I remember yesterday's session," a sleepy face said.

"Then you remember it inaccurately."

The class came to an end and all the pupils, with the exception of the attractive boy, walked outside. She watched him as he moved slowly, as if preparing to make an announcement. He carefully placed his notebook into his beige Eastpak before walking towards the podium.

"Can you give me your email address?" he said. "I want to send along some stuff about Halide Edip Adıvar, which I believe will show you her real character."

"Nothing can change my mind about her. Why are you so obsessed with her anyway? You are here to study English literature. Why talk about a dead Turkish novelist all the time?"

"She is a traitor and she should be known as one."

When he uttered the word "traitor", a cold breeze touched her on the neck.

She wrote down her email address on a piece of paper and wondered whether Halide was merely an excuse for him to hit on her. She feared it was and thought he had the potential to be even ruder than the young assistant.

* * *

Later that evening, when the department was almost empty, he sat next to her and asked whether she had talked to anyone about last night.

She could see it in his eyes. He was more concerned about hiding what had happened between them than in telling people about Halide's ghost. She said she had not told the head of department. He moved his hand, very irritatingly, on to her bra. She told him to take it away and he complied.

She hated him and hated herself for having sex with him, although from a technical standpoint they had only attempted to, thanks to Halide's interruption. After she had made clear that she didn't want to see him that evening, he said he would go to Taksim to meet some friends. She was only happy to get rid of him. After he left she went into the corridor and walked to the bathroom where she looked at the mirror and, to her utter surprise, saw the reflection of the shadow again.

This time she looked older, with a monocle on her face and a cigarette hanging out of her mouth. It was scarier to meet her alone.

"You have this extraordinary talent of concealing essential things in your life," Halide said in a tired voice.

"You manage to hide your affair with that young assistant and nobody seems to realise that you are flirting with your students, which could get you into serious trouble if someone found out. But the thing that irri-tates me the most is your intellectual coward-ice. You are an academic, are you not? Why aren't you telling your pupils about me? You act like a man. They say 'traitor' and you say nothing. Would you say nothing if one of them called a female author a whore?"

She couldn't think of a thing to say.

"You had published an article about me a decade ago. I had read it with great pleasure. But then you got into trouble for it. That was to be expected in a society dominated by male values... You clarified some basic mistakes. You made clear the room where you made love to the young assistant yesterday was not mine. I used to sit on that wooden chair all right, but in 1950s, the department building was in a distant neighbourhood, where I had the wonderful view of the Bosphorus. And you mentioned why I had to go to exile. You were brave enough to tell the truth. But you were not as brave when it came to defending your essay in person. Can you tell me why?"

"I didn't want to frighten my colleagues."

"Frighten them? According to your line of thought, telling the truth, rather than keeping it as a secret, would frighten your colleagues."

"I surely have the freedom to reveal things when I choose."

"You have the freedom to tell the truth, darling, and you also have the freedom to hide it. You chose the latter."

Before she could respond, the head of the Germanic department entered the bathroom and the ghost disappeared, leaving her alone with her face on the mirror.

* * *

→ Before going to sleep that evening she visited her study and read the articles her student had sent to her a few hours earlier. They were written in a particularly nasty tone, in that condescending macho-puritan register. The implication was that Halide was a woman with questionable morals and an unnatural thirst for power. Looking at the computer monitor she was reminded of her early years as an assistant and about how she was treated by her male colleagues and she remembered, too, the tone of their voices. In the faculty corridors and assistants' rooms, she would be reminded by those men about the possibility of her becoming a spinster. They would flirt with her and yet make fun of her status as a single woman. That they could be so comfortable flirting with her despite being married made her sick.

And it was partly as a reaction to them and to the fear of not belonging to their club, that she had taken an interest in Halide and, in the course of one mad August evening 15 years ago, wrote an angry article about her mistreatment. When her colleagues received that article with fury, not to mention a formal warning from the head of department, who said the political atmosphere was not quite right for such truth-digging, she had felt miserable and visited the apartment of an assistant from the Germanic department she had dated a few times. She bore their first child nine months later.

In the darkness of the room, she wondered whether she had done the right thing by visiting him and abandoning Halide, as it

were. As she walked to the door of her study, she suddenly came across the ghost. She was clad in a black burqa and her face looked very young. Her eyes had the most peculiar expression.

"One has to speak out," she said. "When you start speaking out, it turns into a kind of habit. Your mistake was giving it up when you were faced with criticism. You should have continued speaking out. You could have turned it into a habit."

The lights turned on and she saw her husband at the entrance of the room.

"Who are you talking to?"

* * *

The next morning she received a text from the assistant. She didn't know how to respond because it consisted of an explicit sentence, and as she started climbing the endless stairs that led to the faculty floor she thought about the stupidity of the sentence's construction and about how little thought had gone into it. How could she have offered her body to a man with such vile ideas? She was ashamed of herself. The tone of his text was carefully designed to shock and excite her, but it failed on both grounds. Looking at it again the only thing she could think of was Halide's words. She wondered how men managed to speak in this infuriating register. It was the same aggressive, do-as-I-say-or-else tone that had forced her into silence and cunning all those years ago.

She entered the lecture hall and saw the expectant faces of her students.

"Yesterday evening I received an email from one of the members of this class," she said. "The email contained a link to an article that argued that Halide Edip Adıvar, the woman who founded this department, and about whom we had a brief discussion the other day, was a traitor to her nation."

Someone giggled.

"The past few days showed me that this is a belief widely shared by you. Like many contemporaries of Halide you seem to think that this brave woman, the founder of Turkey's PEN club and the author of a number of great novels, should have spent her time at home, rather than become a public intellectual."

There was silence in the room.

"But is it a crime for the artist to become an intellectual and criticise her country when she believes things are going in the wrong direction? As you all know, men are perfectly attuned to following orders. It is often women, or the womanly side in men, that dare criticise what seems wrong and ill-conceived."

The skinny girl smiled at her.

"I want to talk about this woman whom you seem so ready to hate and consider an enemy because you are too scared to question what had been taught to you at high school. First, I shall give you some basic facts. Halide Edip Adıvar was born in 1882 and was educated in an American girls' college in Arnavutköy. She knew Shakespeare by heart. During the occupation of Istanbul by allied forces, which went on for five terrible years, she was one of the leaders of the resistance movement. Instead of writing nasty columns about rebels, Halide became one. She helped organise an uprising and gave a legendary speech to more than 200,000 people in Sultanahmet Square,

which you pass by every day on your way to this faculty. Today it is a tourist site; at the time it was the centre of the uprising. Did anyone tell you about her speech, or the role she had played in the liberation movement? I didn't think so. The history of the Turkish revolution was written by men, after all. Many of those historians were uncritical scribes of the patriarchal discourse. In the eyes of those men, if something was decided then it was perfectly legal to destroy anything that stood in its way. As often happens in this country, women were the first casualties of the realisation of male ambitions."

"As a young woman, she became friends with the leading revolutionary figures and served as their interpreter when foreign journalists came to interview them. She was among the most sophisticated young women in Istanbul. She travelled with the revolutionaries and discussed with them the course of the revolution."

"Can you fast-forward to the point where Halide becomes a traitor?" a voice said. It was him, she knew.

"I cannot because she never became one. That identity was manufactured by men who found her dangerous. After the foundation of the republic Halide campaigned for women's suffrage but she was a lonely figure among male revolutionaries. When she demanded more democracy, and political representation for women, she was told to shut up."

People laughed.

"But they didn't expect what she did next. Halide did not shut up. The lady was not for turning."

→ "What did she do then?"

"She went to London and lived there for more than 15 years. There she became friends with such eminent figures as Bernard Shaw. Columbia University invited her to give a series of lectures and she was more than happy to talk about Turkey and Turkish culture to American audiences. She loved her new role as a visiting lecturer. Her interests had an international scope: she wrote about India's politics and became a popular figure among Indians. She wrote English books and her memoirs were published in England. The

The New York Times hailed her as the face of the modern Turkish woman

New York Times hailed her as the face of the modern Turkish woman."

She told them about the year 1940; about Halide's return to Istanbul and the pleasure she took from her new role as a professor of literature. She told them about her assistants and about her time with the PEN club, and about the wonderful atmosphere she had created in the English literature department. She told them about how some of the most important socialist intellectuals of the country had worked with her, under her patronage. She told them about how, despite her liberal politics, Halide had befriended leftists and tried to protect them when the single-party state started a witch-hunt against them, with the goal of cleaning all socialists from the universities during the1940s.

They listened to her in a state of excitement and disbelief. She hoped they believed her words, but she couldn't tell if they did.

Then she realised she didn't really care about what they thought. After the class came to an end she left the hall and went into the assistants' room. The head of department was there. She asked her whether they could talk in her office.

"Now?" she asked.

"Yes."

* * *

It was the last day of winter. The bedroom overlooking the backstreet was silent. She placed her brow on the window, felt its cold surface on her face and eyed the street. She saw a few cars parked a few metres away from each other. She looked at the large oak tree that she found herself staring at a lot lately. She watched a black cat climb one of its thick branches. She watched her body and the ease with which she moved. Spring had finally come to Istanbul.

The house was empty. She sat on the small bed she had bought for herself last month. Her divorce had been a messy affair but it was worth it – and, when she thought about it later, she knew that it had all begun with Halide's ghost. She had the custody of her daughter and she now wondered what she was doing at school. She had not seen her ghost again after her final appearance in the faculty bathroom but she could feel it continued to move with her. She put on her shoes and felt happy to be alive, although being jobless was not the best companion to a pleasurable state of mind.

But today it could wait. First she would take a walk in the city. She would pass through the areas of Karaköy, Sirkeci and Sultanahmet. She would smell the streets, before deciding on whatever it was she would be doing in the day, whether to spend it alone or with the young neighbour who had asked her out once with the lame excuse of finding out about her favourite author. ☒

© Kaya Genç
www.indexoncensorship.org

Kaya Genç is a novelist and essayist based in Istanbul, Turkey. He tweets @kayagenc

Index around the world

by **Alice Kirkland**

INDEX NEWS

43(2): 186/188 | DOI: 10.1177/0306422014536492

EXCEPTIONAL PEOPLE FIGHTING curbs on free expression across the globe, from Burma to Mexico, were given much-deserved recognition at Index on Censorship's 14th Annual Freedom of Expression Awards in March. Their remarkable, and often shocking, stories were told on big screen at London's arts centre, the Barbican, when Index took over the cinema to host an audience of around 300 journalists, lawyers, artists and other supporters.

Judges, including award-winning playwright Howard Brenton, journalist Samira Ahmed, and Human Rights Silk of the Year 2013 Ed Fitzgerald QC were given the tough task of selecting the winners from incredibly strong shortlist of 17 nominees across four categories: arts, journalism, campaigning and digital activism.

For the first time the Digital Activism Award, sponsored by Google, was voted for online by the public. It drew thousands of votes and, in a surprise twist, Shubranshu Choudhary, from ground-breaking citizen journalism news service CG-Net Swara in India, came out ahead of NSA whistleblower Edward Snowden. Other award winners were independent Azerbaijani newspaper Azadliq, Pakistani digital rights campaigner Shahzad Ahmad and 18-year-old Egyptian rapper Mayam Mahmoud, who treated the audience to a lively performance on the night. Nominees, including Turkish playwright Meltem Arikan and Honduran journalist Dina Meza, also attended the event,

which continued late into the evening in the Barbican's roof gardens. Broadcaster Anna Ford – and former Index chair – declared it "a wonderful awards evening – by far the best ever".

As for Index's own advocacy work, it has also been a busy period, with two key papers produced one on Belarus and one on Brazil. Belarus: Time for Media Reform, launched in February, with three successful events in Minsk, Brussels and London, where videos of first-hand accounts from persecuted Belarusian journalists and activists ran alongside a presentation from the paper's authors, Andrei Bastunets, from the Belarusian Association of Journalists in Minsk, and Index's Andrei Aliaksandrau. The report highlights severe restrictions on media freedom in Belarus, where state-dominated broadcast media and tight controls over print publications have made the country one of the most restrictive and hostile media environments in Europe. It's a frightening situation, which Index will continue to highlight and fight against.

Index has also published a paper on Brazil and internet governance, following a research trip to the country in February by senior advocacy officer Melody Patry. Seizing the momentum of the international forum on the future of internet governance, Net Mundial, which was hosted by Brazil in April, as well as the coming presidential and parliamentary elections, Index met and interviewed a range of journalists, NGOs,, politicians, and internet companies as well as participating in a conference on access to knowledge, education and human rights.

On 23 April, Brazilian president Dilma Rousseff passed the Marco Civil law, providing a legal framework for internet rights, making Brazil the largest country ever to enshrine net neutrality in its legal code. While Brazil has the potential to become a world leader in terms of internet rights, the Index policy paper focused on the main challenges and threats to online freedom of expression in Brazil, as well as the country's increasing role and attitudes in the global internet governance debates. It offers recommendations that challenge restrictions on digital freedom of expression in the country.

Index continues to expand its youth work through a range of on and offline events, schemes and programmes, which have helped to engage young people in the work of Index, while promoting the ideas around free expression. This work has helped Index to bolster our knowledge of what young people believe to be the greatest threats facing their personal freedom of expression.

Tripwires, Index's youth performance programme, held its latest workshop in Newcastle at the Northern Stage theatre. The facilitators worked with the theatre's youth associate company, North, to examine censorship through a series of drama workshops. Alongside this, Index has hosted a number of panel debates on university campuses, including the University of Sussex, giving students the chance to debate with Index staff and fellow students on a variety of censorship issues.

The Index young writers and artists programme launched in March, calling on 16-25 year olds to pitch articles and cartoons for publication on the website, relating to free speech and censorship. There has been an enthsiastic response, and Index has already published 21 contributions. These form part of the new youth platform on the website, which is designed to give young people the

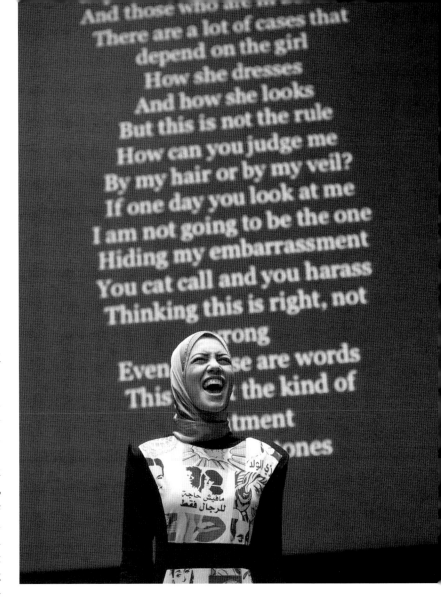

ABOVE: Award winner and singer Mayam Mahmoud raps her acceptance speech at the Index annual awards

opportunity to have their say through social media, interaction at Index debates and via Google Hangouts. Topics already debated

Young writers and artists have responded enthusiastically to the new programme – a chance for 16-25 year olds to pitch articles and cartoons

include homosexuality and the implications of censorship on campus.

For the first time, Index took its magazine on tour to the Leeds Big Bookend literature festival and the Hay Festival, where the debate linked to the Spring issue's special →

→ report on war and propaganda. Panels included Index magazine editor Rachael Jolley, Yorkshire Post journalist Chris Bond, Major Ric Cole, Index chair David Aaronovich and author Chris Paterson, and debated where the line should be drawn on propaganda. Index's editor Rachael Jolley also chaired a debate on freedom in journalism and literature 25 years after the fall of the Berlin Wall at the Prague Book Fair.

Index has also welcomed on board our new chief executive Jodie Ginsberg. Her previous roles include deputy director at think-tank Demos Finance, and as a London bureau chief for Reuters, where she also worked in Ireland and South Africa for a decade as a foreign correspondent and business journalist.

A lot has changed across Europe – and the rest of the world – since the fall of the Berlin Wall 25 years ago, as is charted in this issue's special report, but Index continues to challenge and hold to account those who restrict free speech. ⊠

© Alice Kirkland
www.indexoncensorship.org

Alice Kirkland is an editorial assistant at Index on Censorship

Campus clampdown

END NOTE

43(2): 189/190 | DOI: 10.1177/0306422014536343

US universities are increasingly intolerant of students and have created small free speech zones. **Taylor Walker** reports

WITH FREEDOM OF speech enshrined under the First Amendment, you'd imagine US universities would be the first to uphold a student's rights. And many do – just as long as they don't stray from the proper, designated area, as students from the University Of Hawaii discovered recently when they were prevented from handing out copies of the constitution.

Two students – members of political organisation Young Americans for Liberty – have since filed a lawsuit against the university, claiming they were stopped from distributing handouts during a January event to introduce students to university groups and told they should only do so in a "free-speech zone". "This isn't the 60s anymore," they were allegedly told – a reminder that many such zones were set up as a result of protests over the Vietnam war.

Having specific areas (some of which are marked by lines on the ground and in tucked-away locations) where you can remind people of the First Amendment sounds like a paradox, and many students are questioning their universities on the issue. Earlier this year Robert Van Tuinen received a $50,000 payout after filing a lawsuit against California's Modesto Junior College for stopping him distributing copies of the constitution on Constitution Day. The college is now revising its policy, which says students can only distribute pamphlets in free-speech zones and must also get approval to issue information to the public.

Brandeis University in Massachusetts also came under fire in April, after rescinding an honorary degree due to be awarded to Ayaan Hirsi Ali, the women's rights activist. The university's decision was prompted by Ali's critical remarks on Islam. In a statement defending the decision, officials said Ali's comments were "inconsistent with Brandeis University's core values".

Amanda Pereira, who is taking global studies at Brandeis, says she sometimes feels afraid to raise her hand. "We tend to fear speaking out for fear of repercussions from anyone who has some type of power over us," she says. "As a student your spot is never fully guaranteed."

An annual report released by the Foundation for Individual Rights in Education (Fire) found that more than half of higher education institutions in the US restrict free speech. Brandeis is on the list – as are six of the eight founding universities – for having at least one policy that impedes free expression.

Earlier this year, Yale blocked a student-created course evaluation website, Year Bluebook Plus (YBB+ created as an alternative to the administration-operated site, Yale Bluebook). YBB+, commonly compared to the review site Rate My Professor, was user-friendly and attracted heavy traffic from its inception. When it was shut down, →

→ the university administration's email inboxes were filled with complaints of suppression of free speech – prompting the dean of Yale, Mary Miller, to admit that a review of policies was overdue.

"Technology has moved faster than the faculty could foresee," she said. "What we now see is that we need to review our policies and practices."

During a live chat with the Huffington Post in January, Peter Xu, co-creator of YBB+, said: "This shows that institutions aren't suited for the fast changing pace of technology today. The university's policy is definitely behind the times."

And this isn't something new. Back in 2010, the American Association of Colleges

The college policy said students could only distribute pamphlets in free-speech zones

and Universities conducted a study that sampled 24,000 college students inquiring about freedom of expression on campus. Only 35.6 per cent strongly agreed that "it is safe to hold unpopular opinions on campus".

Yet perhaps the curtailment of free speech in colleges should not come as a surprise. In the mid-1700s, a decade before the Declaration of Independence, the first student protest in America was recorded. The Great Butter Rebellion at Harvard University allegedly began when the grandfather of writer Henry David Thoreau, Asa Dunbar, fervently proclaimed: "Behold, our butter stinketh! Give us, therefore, butter that stinketh not." The protest stirred tension between faculty and students. It also led to the suspension of half the student body. Eventually, the students' demands were met.

Maybe in the 21st century we need more Dunbars on campuses across the nation. Jalem Towler, an undergraduate at Harvard, says students have the tendency to point the

finger at school officials but disregard their own lack of action.

"Administrations don't change culture or negative social norms," says Towler. "It's up to students to speak up and step up when someone's voice is being silenced or restricted."

In an email to Index, Greg Lukianoff, the president of Fire and author of Unlearning Liberty, described the manner in which students self-censor themselves.

"As my experience at Fire can attest, this pessimism is warranted. But students generally avoid getting in trouble by following four simple rules:

1. Talk to the students you already agree with.
2. Join ideological groups that reflect your existing beliefs.
3. Do not disagree with professors whose egos cannot take it.
4. In general, shy away from discussing controversial topics."

"The outward appearance of so many colleges makes everything seem fine but it's really the inner layer that should be heavily exposed," says Pereira.

Challenging the status quo should never be impossible, especially in institutions established to promote inquiry and debate. And although it is saddening that students feel themselves trapped in self-censorship and fear, it takes only one hand and one voice to declare the truth – that restrictions stinketh. ☒

© Taylor Walker
www.indexoncensorship.org

Taylor Walker is a broadcast journalism student at Boston University and tweets @taylorreports